G000043321

NATUZZI

THE
ITALIAN
HARMONY
MAKER

LUCA CONDOSTA

Published by
LID Publishing Limited
The Record Hall, Studio 204,
16-16a Baldwins Gardens,
London EC1N 7RJ, UK

524 Broadway, 11th Floor, Suite 08-120,
New York, NY 10012, US

info@lidpublishing.com
www.lidpublishing.com

A member of:

BPR
Business Publishers Roundtable

www.businesspublishersroundtable.com

© Luca Condosta, 2018
© LID Publishing Limited, 2018

Printed in Great Britain by TJ International
ISBN: 978-1-911498-59-9

Cover and page design: Caroline Li

NATUZZI

THE ITALIAN HARMONY MAKER

LUCA CONDOSTA

LONDON   MONTERREY
MADRID   SHANGHAI
MEXICO CITY   BOGOTA
NEW YORK   BUENOS AIRES
BARCELONA   SAN FRANCISCO

What is love for our work?
It is the chopper who stretches the leather on the table,
who caresses it before cutting
to discover the most invisible defects.
It is the seamstress who opens her eyes to make a straight line.
It is the assembler hugging pillows, dressing them to give them shape.
This is a love that our competitors do not have.

— Pasquale Natuzzi

To my family, friends and colleagues
who have supported me on this journey.
To Pasquale Natuzzi, for giving me a
chance to feel even prouder of my Apulia
while travelling around the world.

CONTENTS

ACKNOWLEDGEMENTS

I have many people to thank for this book:

My parents, my brother and my sister, who always pushed me to strive for excellence without forgetting the real essence of what a family is: a warm place where you can go back and relax without any stress.

Luca, for his patience over these months, watching me surrounded by papers, sketches and listening all my "Wow, they did this and that at Natuzzi etc". You are special to me and, without you, this book would have not been possible. Your big arms have been a safe harbor to shelter when I thought "This book will never be finished".

Vito Basile and Renato Quaranta at Natuzzi Corporate Communication: you were the first people to listen to my ideas about this book and you gave me the trust to proceed. Sharing your time and passion has meant a lot to me and inspired me even further to write this book.

All the people interviewed in the book (Mario Disanto, Gianmichele Pace, Gianni Romaniello, Giuseppe De Santis, Antonio Ventricelli, Nicola Patella, Ing. Lascaro, Joe Stano, Antonio Cavallera, Anna Natuzzi). I hope I was able to give your stories, your memories and your dreams the right visibility.

Sara, Liz, Nikki, Yana and the whole team at LID Publishing for the professionalism and dedication to drive me in this journey, refining every little detail.

Neil, for not reading the manuscript! Now I understand why and I trust your advice, even when you say no to me. I truly believe there's a reason. Just finding it can sometimes be hard.

Andreas, Alex, Peter, Thomas, Knut, Vikas and Stefano: you have been silent spectators waiting for the big opening to happen. I felt your support in life, which helped me progress well on this project.

Heidi who taught me the power of less, the importance of being lean, quick and effective.

The people working at Natuzzi: I met some of you while at the Santer-amo headquarters or during visits to the plants. I have a strong respect for what you have built, for the way you work and I wish you all the best for the future.

Pasquale Natuzzi, I continue to be amazed when I travel around the world and hear people talking about your products. I believe you have created a world, a concept of living and a philosophy of working. You have given the people working for you the most important thing: the dignity of the work. Without compromising on quality and laws, you allowed several generations to live in Apulia, realizing what you call the social mission of Natuzzi. This is not a given from all entrepreneurs. So, thank you from me: I believe this will be the first book where the author asks for the signature of the protagonist rather than the other way round.

The customers of Natuzzi: I realized while writing this book that by buying its products you buy more than a sofa, a table or an armchair. You buy Natuzzi's philosophy and values, you buy the respect for the law and the authentic 'Made in Italy'. When you sit on a Natuzzi sofa, I imagine all the hands who touched that sofa (sewers, designers, carpenters) clapping you on your shoulders and saying thank you for your choice.

The running evenings, the biking mornings and the reading Sundays: I love you all and I need you to balance my brain and to create what I do.

And finally, thanks to all of you who will read this book. I am not a professional writer, but I have a passion for business, sustainability, leadership and in general for stories. We are made of values and when we find a story that deserves to be shared with many people, I believe we have to write it so it doesn't get lost. I hope you enjoy this one.

CHAPTER 1
WHERE IT ALL COMES FROM

It was while traveling for work, something I do often, that I first started thinking about writing a book on Natuzzi. The story of how a small workshop located in a village in Southern Italy transformed itself into a multinational company, selling its products all over the world, was remarkable and very interesting to me.

How can the artisanal production of furniture be transformed into an industrial one, while keeping the manual touch and attention to detail, and also continuing to evoke a sense of harmony and beauty in the consumer?

How can a company with more than 5,000 employees be more known abroad than in its own country?

How is it that a humble team, passionate about their jobs, can realize something that is not feasible on paper, such as listing their company on the New York Stock Exchange?

I have a passion for business and visionary people, and I was intensely curious. So, I emailed Natuzzi's press office and organized a visit to the company.

Natuzzi's headquarters are in Apulia, a southern region of Italy where the sun reflects on white stones, giving the land a red-brownish colour and a unique taste to all its products. In Apulia, concepts such as friendship, trust, honour, family, respect and hard work have a special meaning, and the hardness of the land is reflected in the determination of the people. There is a shared desire to improve, succeed and move up from the stereotype of being the agricultural part of Italy.

When you travel across Apulia, you are surrounded by beauty. You can see it in the landscape, with its Trulli – the traditional dry stone hut with conical roof constructions – or in the ancient typical manor farms surrounded by olive trees. You can feel it when you drink a glass of Negramaro wine, eat taralli and burrata mozzarella, watching the sea and listening to the crickets singing all around.

But you can also be part of it when you get in touch with the local people, who warmly welcome visitors into their lives.

Santeramo in Colle is a small village in Apulia, with fewer than 30,000 inhabitants. It is the highest municipality in the Bari province, located in an area named Bari's Alta Murgia. In this area of ravines, canyons, crypts and sea caves, ancient rupestrian civilization was born. Today, you can find plenty of artisans, vineyards and olive groves. You are close to the ancient Magna Grecia area, where Taranto was the capital, and the influences from that period are still evident in the amazing products and genuine culture.

While driving in this area, my curiosity to understand more about what is behind this company became even stronger. I turned off the radio, opened the car window and started to smell the fragrances in the air and listen to the sounds of nature.

There must be some magic in this small village that guards the history and success of Natuzzi, I thought. In a short period of time, the company has grown to generate work for approximately 5,000 people worldwide, sell its products in over 100 countries and has been recognized as an Italian brand ambassador. These are things that cannot be explained simply through numbers and figures.

Perhaps it has something to do with the beauty and harmony of the place where the company is located. Entering the world of Natuzzi, I found all the answers to my questions.

Pasquale Natuzzi, Chairman and CEO of the Natuzzi Group

CHAPTER 2

THE ORIGINS: THE PERIOD OF DREAMS

(1959–1970)

"I remember having a small laboratory, 3x3m. It was a cupboard more than a laboratory. I woke up at 5am every day and went to work with an incredible passion. I had big dreams, and it was great for me to go to work, even if we did not yet have huge plans for the future.

"That was just 15 years after the war. Poverty and misery were still around me, but working made me a happier person. To me, to imagine an armchair, to realize its frame, to cut the fabric, to sew it and to assemble all the pieces together was an unrepeatable emotion.

"That was a great stage of my life, when my work began, the time I like to recall as the era of my dreams."[1]

Natuzzi's history was not an easy one.

To begin, we need to go back to the 1940s when its founder, Pasquale Natuzzi, was born in Matera, in Southern Italy. The second of seven children, his parents were typical people from that part of the country: his father worked as a carpenter and his mother had a small grocery store. After some years in Matera, the whole family moved to Taranto.

It was shortly after World War II, when even the youngest children had to contribute and support the economy of a family, especially in the south of Italy. At the age of only eight, Pasquale Natuzzi began his day at 5am by helping his mother with milk deliveries. After completing this 'hobby', his day continued at school at 8am, after which he would return to his mother's shop to wash the empty milk bottles. In the late afternoon, he would help his father in his workshop.

Although this was a period of renaissance for the Italian economy, it was not an easy life.

Time passed and Pasquale helped his family, acquiring values of honour, respect, dedication and hard work.

---

1   Pasquale Natuzzi in *Crescere Insieme* 2000, vol. 34

Once he was 15, Pasquale felt a desire to do something more. He decided to become an apprentice at a friend's upholstering workshop. He started an educational journey to simply understand how to build the wooden structure of a sofa. He would watch and admire the artisanal work, the dexterity of hands, the gestures and the dedication that craftsmen put into their work to create a unique piece.

It was during this time that Pasquale Natuzzi fell in love with what was to become the work of his entire lifetime: the design and creation of magnificent sofas.

In 1959, having been in this workshop for two years, Pasquale decided to open his own artisanal space in Taranto for producing sofas and arm-chairs. At first, he only had a second-hand sewing machine, a hammer and four scissors to create his sofas. But, more importantly, he had great passion for his work.

In those early days, margins were tight and profits were very low. Following the advice of a family friend, Pasquale realized that 90kms away, in Matera, there was a lack of upholsterers, and he decided to move his shop there in 1962. His three employees moved with him at first, but soon felt homesick and decided to go back, leaving Pasquale alone again.

He was a man driven by passion, but this change in the situation limited the new venture and put him in a difficult position. Sometimes, passion alone is not sufficient to transform dreams into reality, although it can help you move forward. Pasquale recognized that he could either continue alone or change his plans. Having realized the need for furniture shops in Matera, he decided to convert his business into a furniture trade business instead.

Unfortunately, this wasn't as successful as he had hoped and, after only five years, the shop closed down with a loss of 143 million Italian Lira (ITL), equivalent to around €74,000. This left Pasquale with a lot of debt and limited credit.

Despite suffering this defeat on his first attempt to work in the Italian sofa market, Pasquale still had a high level of curiosity about the work.

In 1967, he decided to go back to his first love and produce sofas, rather than simply selling them. In that year, he financed Natuzzi Salotti, a small company that specialized in producing upholstery fabrics, with three employees.

Finally, after numerous challenges, this decision paid off. The company expanded from a production capacity of 25 seats per day in 1967 to 100 seats[2] per day and 20 employees just two years later, which increased again to 45 in 1973.

The effective growth of the company meant the workshop in Matera no longer had the capacity to host the operations, and a new workshop was needed. Pasquale decided to move all operations to Santeramo in Colle, in the region of Apulia. Here he found interest and understanding from local administrators and bought a piece of land on which he started the construction of a large new plant, 3,000 square metres.

Initially, the idea was to move to Apulia after the construction of the new plant had been fully completed. But, in reality, the move happened suddenly and rather traumatically. On 11 August, 1973, a few days before the summer break, a circuit breaker in a car parked in the Matera workshop's courtyard generated a fire. The workshop was destroyed and everything was lost: money, accounting records, invoices, everything except vendors' records.

While the insurance coverage was approximately 38 million ITL[3], the estimated damages totalled approximately 200 million ITL.

After such devastation, it's not always easy to start again. Some would easily give up or decide to change their approach to life. Instead, Pasquale invited all the employees to meet him at a Natuzzi exhibition shop in Mater – the only available space they had – the day after the fire.

---

2   'Seat' is used as unit of measurement in sofa and armchair production. A sofa usually consists of three seats, while an armchair consists of one seat.

3   After two years, the insurance indemnified only 28 million ITL, able to cover just the legal expenses.

At that meeting, they decided to roll up their sleeves – literally. They disassembled the sofas, in order to save the component templates, and started to work in the new plant. At that time, the new plant was still under construction, with no equipment, no doors or even windows.

"One week after the fire, we started producing again. Some people left the company, but I could not. I believed in my job and in the charisma of Pasquale Natuzzi. I was hired for 90,000 lire, a fortune … I had a strong love for the company and, like someone you love, I could not leave it. We all worked together to get the company back on its feet again.

I remember that in September of that year, Pasquale was not able to pay our salaries, but I got my salary back the next month, even though the company had been destroyed,"[4] recalled Nicola Patella, a Natuzzi employee for 47 years.

Typically August is a time when everybody in Italy is away on their summer break, so there was no help from the surrounding companies.[5] Matters got worse when a local newspaper reported that Pasquale could not prove he still had money to collect from his customers, which resulted in 80% of them not paying their debts.

On top of all this, it happened to be a particularly rainy summer in Santeramo that year. So, to protect the material in the new plant (which was still under construction), everything had to be covered with plastic sheets. Pasquale decided to sleep inside the new plant for three months. Thanks to his determination and the willingness of his employees, production started just 17 days after the fire, and they were able to deliver the first load of orders, which was for 1,760,000 ITL and paid in cash.

On that day, Pasquale decided to call all of his employees and start a new fire. This time the fire was used to light up a barbecue to celebrate their contributions and to look forward to the future with one strong belief: *"We start again, stronger than ever."*[6]

---

4   Nicola Patella, an employee at Natuzzi for 47 years, interviewed in January, 2017.

5   Castelli M., "L'uomo del sud che da lavoro al nord", Il Sole 24 Ore, 11 May, 2000.

6   Crescere Insieme n. 34, Luglio 2000, page 22.

Pasquale Natuzzi as a child (left) with his family

Pasquale Natuzzi at the national skating championship, 1958

The first workshop in Taranto, 1959

The Santeramo in Colle manufacturing plant under construction, 1972

CHAPTER 3

THE YEARS OF SACRIFICE

(1970–1986)

"The period between the 1970s and mid-1980s is what I called the period of sacrifices. At the beginning of those years, we made tremendous sacrifices. We could not be where we are today without our extraordinary people. We had to overcome incredible adversities, and I always told my employees: 'Guys, we can do it, we must do it by ourselves!' The alternative was to go to Germany or Switzerland and queue, together with plenty of other people, to get a job. We invented a way to produce sofas, and we created work."[7]

In the mid-1970s, Pasquale realized the limits of distribution in Italy, as it was very fragmented and therefore difficult to penetrate the market successfully. This set-up did not allow producers to plan growth effectively. So he began to consider expanding into foreign markets, attending furniture fairs and forming relationships with key distributors there.

He attended the first fair in 1975 in Bari and established connections with customers in the Middle East. However, at that time, the Middle East was not considered a stable market, both politically and economically. This pushed Pasquale to expand his geographic boundaries elsewhere.

A second opportunity came along in 1977 at the International Interior Fair in Cologne, Germany. It was a big expense to exhibit, and Pasquale could only afford a 12m² booth to showcase his product, which in practical terms meant only one sofa. He chose to show a leather sofa called Navaho, which was a new product for Natuzzi – since production was mainly focused on fabric – but able to meet the demands of European customers.

Even though he only had one product on display, and the fact that it was a leather product was slightly risky, the fair proved a success for Pasquale. Among the exhibitors he met was a Belgian furniture distributor with a chain of stores, Universe du Cuir, which specialized in leather sofas. The relationship between Natuzzi and Universe du Cuir was immediately established, both relatively young companies, eager to succeed and keen to work together. After a few months, 60% of Natuzzi's orders where coming from this Belgian distributor.

---

7   Pasquale Natuzzi in *Crescere Insieme*, vol. 35, page 20.

Foreign markets were, without a doubt, the area to focus on, but Pasquale's limited knowledge of English hindered this expansion. For this reason, he decided to fly to London in 1979 and learn what would become his second language: English.

The company kept growing, and in 1980 it achieved 6 million ITL in revenue and had approximately 100 employees. Meanwhile, following the demand from the Belgian market, the company shifted its focus to leather sofa production, which became 50% of its overall revenue and eventually 100% of production by 1981.

Given the valuable customer relationship Universe du Cuir had forged with Natuzzi, they were keen to cultivate this further and were eager to become Natuzzi's exclusive distributor in the majority of European countries. However, Pasquale saw another potential opportunity and took a risk by refusing this offer to focus, instead, on the American market. This was a risky decision, and it resulted in the termination of all contracts with the Belgian counterpart. Additionally, it was a difficult time for the furniture sector. The Middle Eastern markets had collapsed, and there was a decline in domestic demand due to the economic downturn.[8]

Pasquale very quickly felt the pressure of the imminent need to find a new market for his products.

He visited the Americas for the first time in 1980, when he attended a furniture fair in Montreal, Canada. It was more of a generic trade fair, but he didn't want to miss the opportunity to fly there and taste the appetite for his products in the biggest market in the world.

Once in Montreal, he realized the fair was, *"nothing more than a farm fair,"* and there was not much point staying, so he decided to travel to New York and visit some of the big department stores. A nice summary of this episode was written by Peter Fuhrman in *Forbes*.[9]

"Having entered a Macy's store, Pasquale noted that the unbranded leather sofas were priced at $2,999, which seemed quite expensive to the Italian entrepreneur. 'I was already selling $10 million worth of leather furniture

a year in Europe, and my wholesale price was under $500.' While browsing the store, he decided to bet on the possibility of producing better sofas for half this price and, in his broken English, Pasquale successfully convinced a Macy's sofa buyer to look at Natuzzi's quote for three-seat leather sofas.

On his return to Santeramo, Pasquale calculated the cost of shipping and customs duties payable in the US and quoted a lump sum price of $445 per sofa – although this was a rather aggressive pricing for Natuzzi, he saw the opportunity and risk, and he wanted the business. And he got it. Macy's placed an order for 100 sofas, which sold out almost overnight for $999 each."

In an article in the *Wall Street Journal*,[10] Lisa Bannon also recorded an interesting story about Pasquale Natuzzi's tenacity when approaching a big player such as Macy's.

"When R. H. Macy & Co. considered buying leather sofas from an unknown Italian manufacturer in 1982, the buyers posed one condition: they would place an order from Industrie Natuzzi SpA, but only in return for exclusivity in the New York area. 'I said no, you can't tell me how to run my business. I am going to sell to whomever I want,' recalled Pasquale Natuzzi. 'Nobody was producing volumes at my prices.'"

It was during this time that Pasquale matured his instinct and idea: the lower price point would allow anyone in America to buy a contemporary leather sofa of outstanding value, as well as the option to choose from a selection of colours and models that would cater to the needs of any customer.

The success in America ignited an explosive element for Natuzzi. The market wanted more and more from the brand: more models, more colours and in higher volumes.

---

8   Sinisi A., "Natuzzi. Un divano a Wall Street", Egea, 2008.

9   Fuhrman, Peter, "Leather Man," *Forbes*, 7 November 1994, pp. 296-297.

10   Bannon, Lisa. "Natuzzi huge selection of leather furniture pays off," *The Wall Street Journal*, 17 November 1994.

"I remember the beginning in America was not easy. Americans maintained that our sofas were not robust enough. I was working on prototypes at that time and I created one with the skeleton in iron. One episode, which is still clear in my mind, happened during a fair in the US: Mr Natuzzi took a knife and cut the sofa in two, showing the structure to all visitors. This was met with enthusiasm – I remember we sold I don't know how many of that model … we were struggling on how to further produce it!" recalled Nicola Patella.[11]

In the years up to 1985, Natuzzi grew exponentially to around 150 employees, revenues of 42 billion ITL and four times its production capacity.

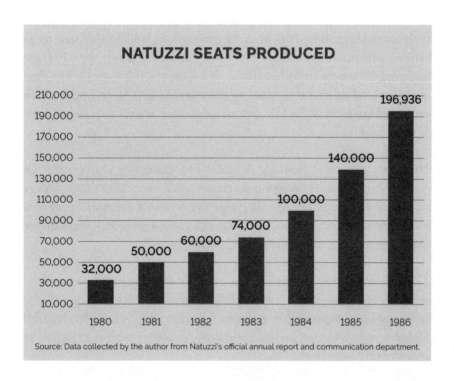

Source: Data collected by the author from Natuzzi's official annual report and communication department.

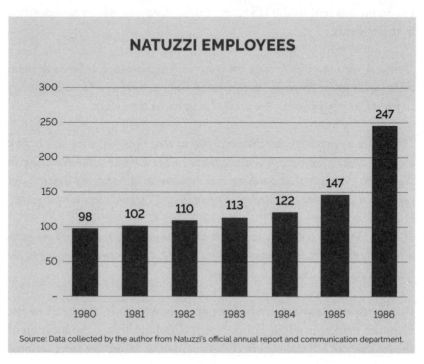

Source: Data collected by the author from Natuzzi's official annual report and communication department.

International furniture fairs played a great role in helping Pasquale forge connections and relationships with other markets. Initially the two main furniture fairs were in Milan (Italy) and Cologne (Germany). But Pasquale decided to attend as many of the relevant fairs as he could, which generated business in the UK, Spain, Belgium, France, Germany and the Middle East.

"Since its beginning, Pasquale Natuzzi was focused on interpreting the customers' needs and, although some models could seem weird in the Italian market, he was producing sofas as the market requested. I remember one time a customer asked for a four-seater sofa and eight armchairs," recalled Joe Stano, current Natuzzi Customer Care Director. [12]

To sustain growth, the focus was also on reshaping the commercial network, the production and logistic structures. Macy's required the company to be registered in order to sell sofas and so, in 1985, Natuzzi Upholstery Inc. was set up – a commercial company with the mission of coordinating sales in the US.

Joe Stano was sent to the US to start this adventure, which he described in these words:

"Initially the idea was to open an office in San Francisco, where our main distribution agent for America was based. But, in order to set up a completely independent organization, we decided to go to the East Coast.

"Thanks to a connection Mr Natuzzi had at that time, we were able to find a corner apartment with seven windows in the Empire State Building in New York. My initial assignment was expected to last only six months, but the American market exploded in our hands, and I stayed there for six years.

"Living there and watching customers who immediately recognized the commerciality of an Apulia product gave me a sense of pride and belonging to the company that was and still is priceless." [13]

By that time, the company had set up a showroom in the heart of the furniture market in High Point, North Carolina. This is the location of the majority of US upholstery companies and is where the International

Home Furnishing Market takes place twice a year. Natuzzi's managers were visiting two to four times a year to manage customers and fairs, so this was clearly not the ideal set-up.

This massive success also affected production, which was still based on the artisanal work of people in Apulia and partially on external contractors. This set-up was not ideal to sustain growth. It could not guarantee the full control of the value chain and might generate delays, lack of quality and inefficiencies in production.

For this reason, in 1986, Pasquale started the vertical integration of his value chain, through the direct control of the entire production, from raw materials and semi-finished goods to creation in Santeramo.

To be more effective and also be able to show the customer the product first-hand, the office was moved to High Point in 1987, close to the showroom.

"The way this relocation was managed makes me proud, since we were able to move activities to the new office without losing a single contract, working in parallel with the two structures in a period where the internet was not available and all the commercial work was done through fax, telex or phone. For ten days we worked in parallel, offering a bonus to the people working in New York in order to ensure a smooth handover to their colleagues in High Point."[14]

This new set-up helped place Natuzzi in a position where it controlled 92% of the materials and goods needed to produce sofas.

The decisions to focus on exports, specialize in leather sofa production, and vertical integration of the value chain were key to Pasquale's and Natuzzi's success. Although these decisions were originally made in the 1980s, even today they are still practised and instrumental to the success of Natuzzi.

---

12   Joe Stano, interview performed in January 2017.
13   Ibid.
14   Ibid

Navaho, The leather sofa presented at the 1977 Cologne Furniture Fair

CHAPTER 4

THE YEARS OF ALTRUISM

ALTRUISM

(1986–1993)

"Between the mid-1980s and 1993 is what I call the period of altruism. Our company was significantly growing and, during our Christmas dinners, I was always taking stock of the overall situation. Many times I asked myself, 'Next year, what shall we do? Shall we go on holiday? Shall we buy a big car, now that we are rich … ' but then I looked around me and there were still people looking for jobs. So, I was still seeing opportunity for growth and I was telling myself, 'We can still grow, we must reinvest the money into the company, building new plants, hiring new people, exploring new markets …'"[15]

The process of vertical integration continued in 1987 when Natuzzi first acquired IMPE, a company located close to Naples, specializing in the production of polyurethane foam. IMPE was able to transform polyurethane and make it usable in sofas.

But to complete the integration, another piece of the value chain needed to be considered, and that was the leather.

The northeastern part of Italy had a great tradition of leather tanning. And that was where Natuzzi started looking for a leather production company to purchase. Natuzzi came across a suitable family-run company, called Cogolo, and acquired it. The acquisition involved changing the name to Natco and rebuilding its production processes to increase efficiency and enable further integration with the Natuzzi way of working.

At the time of the acquisition, Natco had 70 employees. That number rose to 300 in only a few years.

This acquisition was exactly what Natuzzi's engine needed to power up and move its growth forward with full speed. The focus on production optimization and 'just-in-time' techniques were the key factors involved in minimizing the need to stock masses of raw material, eliminating the need to warehouse finished goods and increasing the speed of production.

---

15 Pasquale Natuzzi in Crescere Insieme, vol. 36, page 23.

Although these were years of growth and expansion for Natuzzi, they were also the years of the Gulf War and a period of recession and economic crisis in the US. For a short time, this affected the revenue growth Natuzzi had previously experienced, but it picked up again soon after 1990.

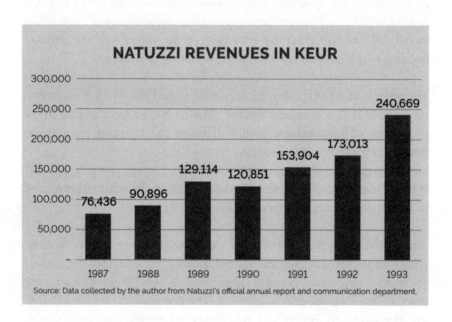

NATUZZI REVENUES IN KEUR

Source: Data collected by the author from Natuzzi's official annual report and communication department.

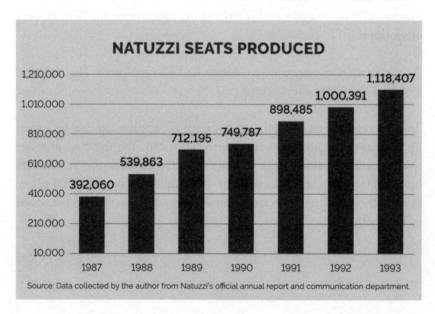

NATUZZI SEATS PRODUCED

Source: Data collected by the author from Natuzzi's official annual report and communication department.

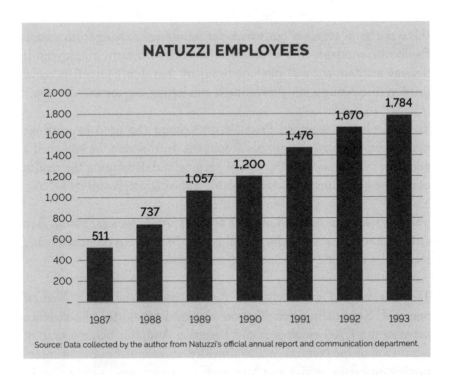

NATUZZI EMPLOYEES

Source: Data collected by the author from Natuzzi's official annual report and communication department.

Overall, revenue grew by 215%, from 76 million euros in 1987 to 241 million euros in 1993. In addition, the number of seats produced increased from 392,000 to 1.1 million, and the number of employees increased from 511 to 1,784.

In regard to the sales of its products, Natuzzi's key success factors included its contemporary designs and the medium–low price range offered. These were the optimal factors for retail chains and, as a result, 66% of revenue came from contracts with big American stores: Macy's, Bloomingdale's, Dillard's, Sears, Seaman's, Levitz (furniture stores) and other specialized stores.[16]

It was a fervent time of growth in which the company demonstrated its capacity to share wellness, create new economies and generate new jobs and business opportunities in the territory where it operated. Notably,

---

16 Sinisi A., "Natuzzi. Un divano a Wall Street," Egea, 2008.

this was a 'grow together' era, when Natuzzi started moving from a small family-run company to a structured company with many employees. It became a structured and modern company that didn't forget its social mission of creating a job, protecting it and letting it grow and develop.

To keep all this together, Pasquale understood the need to continue openly communicating with his employees. In this vein, he launched a company magazine, with the aim of keeping and developing the wealth of relations on which Natuzzi was born and which represent its DNA.

The first issue was released in 1991 and was titled, *Natuzzi Planet*. But, after an internal survey (which resulted in 376 different proposals being received) a new title was selected: *Grow Together*.

The idea worked extremely well for the context in which Natuzzi operated. Essentially, *Grow Together* managed to shorten the distance between the 1,700 employees and Pasquale. And, this being a time of rapid growth for Natuzzi, it also provided an essential outlet of information on opportunities and how each employee was instrumental in taking care of Natuzzi – their own company. The in-house magazine informed employees how their behaviour impacted customers' perceptions of the company, its revenues and, therefore, its net profit.

The company culture began to slowly surface more and more, built on the values of trust, recognition of merit, and mutual commitment – that was commitment from the owner and also from the employees to preserve and guarantee their ongoing prosperity.

The Need for Change in Natuzzi's Human Resource Management

Employees played a pivotal role in helping Natuzzi deliver the desired results. But having to nurture a force of more than 1,700 employees required a more professional approach to their management.

In 1991, a plan was established to organize and provide training sessions to help facilitate the learning curve and bring employees up to full speed.

Ad hoc training sessions were also organized for the management and department heads (IT training, management techniques and language training), teaching them new skills that would be useful for a new mindset at Natuzzi. The aim was to ensure "a distributed but also consistent growth" in the whole organization.[17]

With the growth of Natuzzi, the entire production cycle grew and was managed through 12 companies in total:

- Four companies dedicated to sofa production (Natuzzi Salotti, Softaly, Diellesse, Italsofa)
- Three companies dedicated to the production and transformation of polyurethane foam needed for padding sofas (IMPE, Natex, Tecnolevante)
- Two companies dedicated to leather tanning (Natuzzi Pelle and Natco)
- Three companies dedicated to developing the distribution channels (Natuzzi Americas and Natuzzi Mobili).

Some employees were heavily influenced by the contagious entrepreneurial spirit that Pasquale demonstrated. They became involved in these new sister/daughter companies and maintained a connection to Natuzzi productions.

Natuzzi's Growth and Its Three Pillars for Success
One factor that helped to drive Natuzzi's growth was its productivity. Using a very basic ratio (number of seats/number of employees), Natuzzi was able to double its productivity over the years, passing from 326 seats per employee in 1980 to 627 seats per employee in 1993.

---

17   Crescere Insieme, vol 1, pp. 26-41.

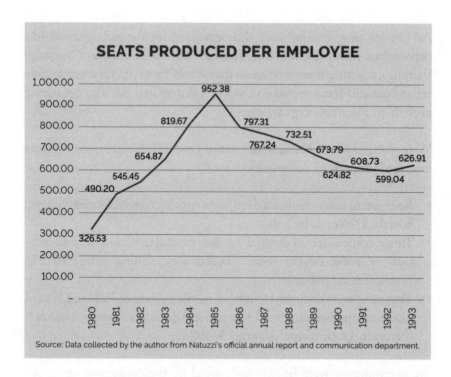

SEATS PRODUCED PER EMPLOYEE

326.53, 490.20, 545.45, 654.87, 819.67, 952.38, 797.31, 767.24, 732.51, 673.79, 624.82, 608.73, 599.04, 626.91

Source: Data collected by the author from Natuzzi's official annual report and communication department.

At the heart of Natuzzi's strategy are three pillars that have expedited its success: innovation, quality and efficiency. Collectively, these helped it to maintain its position worldwide, despite being a local company in an area with poor infrastructure and relatively high labour costs.

Innovation was embedded into the production from the very first stages. From 1991, research and development (R&D) became a key consideration for Natuzzi, who assigned approximately 100 specialized employees to scour the market, identify and translate customers' needs into products. Natuzzi's flexibility allowed them to work with their retail customers and design certain models that would work best in their specific markets. Market needs, combined with customer specifications, were and still are today the key ingredients that enable Natuzzi to develop a successful product.

Skilled craftsmanship, combined with meticulous material selection and attention to detail, is what allowed ideas to materialize from the creatives at Natuzzi.

Two of the most experienced prototype developers refer to the creative process of inventing a sofa by saying it is *"a relationship similar to the woman you love. First you have courtship, whether it lasts a short or long time, and only then do you get the satisfaction of the first yes."*[18]

Quality was not implemented in a silo approach – department by department – but, at Pasquale's insistence, was a part of the day-to-day considerations. To maintain high quality standards, Pasquale put the customer at the centre and aimed all the company's processes towards customer satisfaction. His approach was well recognized and appreciated.

Computer-aided design (CAD) systems and internal procedures were introduced to help employees find errors, including problems with materials, in order to prevent quality issues in the final product. In 1992, this led to a big shift in how Natuzzi monitored quality, in that quality checks were conducted not only at the end of the production, but also at the beginning of it, when materials were received. This new, more stringent approach facilitated a reduction of waste or nonconformity at the end of the production.

Efficiency started with the R&D department. After a prototype had been created, designers and artisans together simulated its production in a demo plant to measure the production time and the quantity of materials needed. All this was necessary to plan the production and ensure the product instructions allowed a standardization of an artisanal product without losing the attention to detail.

The first editions of *Grow Together* revealed how maniacal the calculation for average times of production – and measurement of materials required to produce them – was. "Productivity is our insurance towards the future," they said at Natuzzi[19] at this time.

Productivity and efficiency were also obtained through the already mentioned 'just-in-time' production approach, a complicated puzzle for

---

18   Crescere Insieme, vol. 1 par 92, page 2.
19   Crescere Insieme vol 3. Oct 1992, page 5.

production planning every week based on the orders received and the time available at each plant. Working in this way, by time saturation, ensured that each plant operated at its maximum efficiency level.

In addition, the supply chain department played a significant role in Natuzzi's productivity and efficiency. Through its complex system, which allowed raw materials to reach the plants exactly when they were in need, it began by taking into account the order confirmation by the customer and, the delivery date agreed upon, it would plan the production of the model purchased and all resources needed to make it happen and transform the customer dream into reality.

Looking back, Natuzzi was unrecognisable to when it first started out in 1959. After understanding the need to move away from a one-man company to become an organization with numerous employees, Natuzzi developed a structure and workforce that easily had the capacity to evolve even further.

This can be regarded as the first revolution of Natuzzi. From an informally grown company to a more self-aware company, a structured and organized multinational organization, made of an aggregation of several other companies, with a functional structure and an overarching committee that coordinate all activities within the group. *"He formed a very solid team from the human point of view, leaving a lot of freedom to the individuals to express themselves and generate an impact,"* recalled Pietro Lascaro, former director of production. [20]

In the previous years, Pasquale was involved not only in the design of each model, but in all decision-making that was concerned with the industrial and commercial strategies. In the 90s, he was still the final decision maker, but led with his executive team and his two daughters, Annunziata and Annamaria, who had both been with the company since the beginning.

---

20   Pietro Lascaro, interview performed in January 2017.

It was during these years that the decision was made to create a wider delegation process concerning responsibility and decision-making. This was needed to ensure the company could adapt its structure and sustain growth on a global scale.

Within the priorities identified in this plan, there was a need to prepare the company for processing higher volumes, increasing delegation, strengthening marketing and sales, and establishing a structured planning and control system.

TABLE 1: NATUZZI BUSINESS PLAN 1990-1994 – KEY COMPONENTS[21]

MAIN STRENGTHS

- US market leadership
- Niche production
- Market know-how
- Vertical integration
- Innovation
- Learning curve
- Financial solidity

MAIN WEAKNESSES

- Small family-run company
- Low level of delegation and inadequate organizational structure
- Heavy dependency on one market
- Single product

TARGETS

- **Products**: increase overall quality; verify possibility to differentiate leveraging on fabric and classic style
- **Markets**: keep presence in North America; strengthen Europe and Italy presence; leverage possibility to expand in Far East; entry in the high-price upholster markets
- **Competitive strategy**: start competing on quality and corporate image; keep cost competition in consolidated markets; differentiate to get critical mass in markets with low growth

ACTIONS

- **Products**: innovative design to improve quality, gain efficiency in assembly and in raw material usage; enlarge the collection

- **Production and logistics**: leather tanning process integration; rationalization of productive units and warehouses

- **Organization**: improve organization to manage the high volumes; delegation; strengthening marketing and sales department; establish a structured system of planning and control

- **Market and distribution**: consolidate relationships with distributors; increase number of sales agents in all areas; verify opportunity to diversify distribution channels in different markets

- **Financials**: to be listed; self-financing; reduction of production costs

---

21   Sinisi A., "Natuzzi. Un Divano a Wall Street," Egea, 2008.

This new structure was still functional, but enabled every director to have more power and for new departments to be introduced (legal, human resources and organization, information systems, finance, logistics, supply chain, sales and marketing).

The first executive committee was also established. Pasquale took the role of president and CEO, and young managers, including Giuseppe Desantis, became part of it.

Giuseppe joined Natuzzi in 1984 as a clerk in the accounting department. After many years, covering several positions, he was promoted to the corporate reporting and planning department in 1990 and went on to even higher positions with time and experience under his belt.

There are several similar stories of internal growth at Natuzzi, demonstrating that hard work, sharing the values of the company and dedication paid off for Natuzzi employees.

Another example is Giuseppe Vito Stano, who joined Natuzzi in the export area of the business in 1980 and, within that year, became the vice president of Natuzzi Americas before becoming sales and marketing director.

To motivate employees and prevent unproductiveness, Michele Bonerba, HR director, encouraged all employees to roll their sleeves up in order to make Natuzzi *"the world leader in upholstered furniture production."* Michele created his own formula of unproductiveness:

Unproductiveness = Personnel absences + Production deficit

In doing so, Michele created a tool that would set in place healthy competition across the different plants, where the results of the formula would be shared and clearly show which plants were operating at the expected level and which were not.

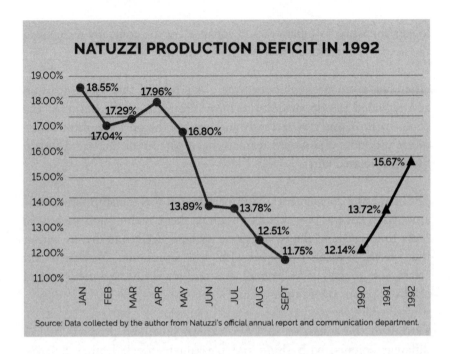

NATUZZI PRODUCTION DEFICIT IN 1992

Source: Data collected by the author from Natuzzi's official annual report and communication department.

This focus on growth was also evident in Natuzzi's balance sheets. The company's equity rose from 3 million euros in 1986 to around 33 million euros in 1993. This reflected Pasquale's typical Italian approach, being a man who wants to save money for the grey moments. Rather than distributing dividends, the profit was reinvested into the operations, R&D and new plants.

To make the message even stronger, Michele quantified the impact of lost revenues due to unproductiveness (i.e., in 1992, 8,500 sofas were not produced due to personnel absences, additionally more than 14,000 sofas were not produced due to production opportunities not being optimal, which equated to approximately 43 billion ITL lost in revenue) in the company's *Grow Together* magazine.

During those years, the company also deliberated over its geographic footprint. There was evident risk behind the heavy dependencies Natuzzi had on the US market. At that time, 90% of all revenues were attributed to this market, which meant that if the US economy crashed, or if American consumers suddenly chose not to buy Natuzzi products any longer, the whole company would collapse. So, the company recognized the need to penetrate a wider worldwide market.

Attending commercial fairs became a key part of this transformation and provided the opportunity to move the focus of the business. The company took this very seriously and became the only upholstered furniture producer that would regularly take part in all the world's main furniture-related fairs.

The marketing department played a key role in this transformative initiative. Each fair was researched through market screening and analysis in order to understand the customer behaviours, needs and drivers within that specific market. Equipped with this information, Natuzzi would create new models, new technologies and an entire new collection of products before attending any fair.

Further to this initiative, in 1993 Natuzzi presented products in 135 different colours, with shiny and pleasant-to-touch leather finishes, and customers could choose the specifications to their preferences. This offering had an indisputable impact on the market and sales.

Thanks to these efforts, in 1993 Natuzzi's geographic footprint achieved a healthier spread and its revenue generation in the US decreased from 92% to 50%. The rest was gained in territories such as France, the UK and Germany.

To effectively penetrate the various markets, Natuzzi's commercial department was organized in five geographic areas: the Americas; Germanic countries and Switzerland; France, Benelux and Iberia Peninsula; Italy; UK, Ireland and Scandinavia, together with the rest of the world. In total, Natuzzi had 50 people working globally on the commercial structure.

In each region, a sales director was appointed to be the 'eyes and the ears' of Natuzzi. Each one would put in place the commercial strategy in their territories, but also look out for market needs and changes, and communicate all such information to the central marketing department in Santeramo, which then had the required insight to refine strategies.

Having a look at the internal market, we can say that the Italian market was both a pleasure and a pain for Pasquale. In 1993, Natuzzi's revenues in its own country were around 136 billion ITL, with around 700 customers, while in the US, Natuzzi's revenues were 20 times more, with half the number of customers.

Pasquale still had one question: *"What about Italy? Why can't I sell my sofas here?"*

The Italian furniture market operated in a totally different way, with a different mentality, very resistant to change. There were more than 28,000 independent shops, selling different types of products from different producers. But the most important characteristic was that the large majority of these shops were owned by small family companies.

Giuseppe Desantis refers to the Italian market as *"asphyxiated, dispersed, and a family fragmented distribution network that does not suit the Natuzzi vision of high artisan products with an industrial logic that are sold in large quantities.*

"Large quantities are not manageable in the Italian market. Whereas in the US we reach ten times the volume that we do in Italy with fewer than half the customers. To this we also need to add the high administrative cost for managing each Italian purchase (one order, one item, one invoice, several bank draft/bills and a very low value to invoice ratio, replicated many times for each order we get in Italy, compared to big orders we get from US distributors with a value to invoice ratio at least 100 times greater). "[22]

So, there were only really two options available for the Italian market: either cope with the market as it was or take courage and act. Natuzzi chose to take action and reinvented itself.

From a starting point of 12 agents managing 700 shops, Pasquale began to toy with the idea of using an alternative distribution method. This was a reflection of what he had observed happen to the French furniture

---

22   Giuseppe Desantis, interview performed in January 2017.

distribution market, where there was a much more dynamic distribution through chain stores.

This was the birth of Divani&Divani, the brand through which Natuzzi sells its sofas all around Italy, with a franchising formula very well known in the rest of Europe. The name itself, translated into English, is Sofa&-Sofa and was chosen as it combines the possibility of selling both leather and fabric sofas, because the Italian market did not favour leather sofas as much as other territories.[23]

The first shop opened in Taranto in 1990 and initially started off with 90% leather sofas and only 10% fabric sofas. *"After a few months, we realized the leather was way more appreciated and we decided to take a chance on it,"*[24] reports Gianmichele Pace, former marketing director at Natuzzi.

Six months later, the company decided to terminate the existing commercial relationships with traditional Italian distributors and created an expansion plan with Divani&Divani. Only two years later, two new shops opened, one in Milan and the other in Saronno. And, in 1993, the number of Divani&Divani stores had risen to 20, with plans to open an additional 60 stores.

The year 1993 was a pivotal one for Natuzzi and marked the start of a new era, when Natuzzi became recognized worldwide by just three letters: NTZ. This was the symbol given to Natuzzi by the New York Stock Exchange after the company conducted its initial public offering.

The Birth of the Murgia District

During these years, a high number of companies in Apulia started following the growth and development of Natuzzi. All these companies were part of the wider Murgia industrial district.

---

23 Gianmichele Pace, interview performed in January 2017.
24 Ibid
25 Marshall A. (1920) *Principles of Economics*, Macmillan and Co.: London.

In economic theory, when we talk about an industrial district, we generally refer to a conglomerate of manufacturing companies all located in the same area, all of which tend to be specialized in the production of products that are similar or even exactly the same.

This is in line with the first definition given by Marshall[25] in 1922. The economist studied the development of the local production system in England, highlighting how the birth and evolution of a district are closely related to what he called *'industrial atmosphere'*.

In these economic realities, a strong interpenetration between the economy and the social experience is at the base. Mixed with a bourgeois enterprise, craftsmanship and strong associative spirit, it is then competition between all players, including entrepreneurs and workers who operate in the same district.

The artisan vocation is the key peculiarity of an industrial district, which tends to not exceed certain dimensions and develops an entire internal competitiveness that allows growth, but also an increase in production quality.

As operators acquire specific skills typical to the district, it is not uncommon that they decide to separate from the original nucleus that gave impetus to their development with new business cells, which help to maintain high-level competition.

The geographical dimension is also interesting for a district. The area in which the district is developing is well defined, but not completely crystallized within its borders that are iridescent, fractal of a changing system.

It lives not only in the working area, but also in the social structure that forms the basin. In the vast majority of cases, families form a miniature reproduction of a business model that is similar to that seen in the 70s, fathers and sons employed in the same company.

The main ingredients of an industrial district are: a well-defined social context, a territory within which the companies operate and a know-how of craft skills that relate to a reference product.

Looking at the industrial district of the upholstered sofa, in Southern Italy it was confined in the geographic triangle formed by the city of Matera and the villages of Altamura and Santeramo in Colle.

Natuzzi was the first company in the area that produced medium- to high-quality leather sofas with vast possibilities for customization at lower prices than global competitors.

The growth of Natuzzi was heavily influenced by the presence of skills and know-how in these areas, and in particular in carpentry, knitting and leatherwork. All these helped trigger the endogenous process within the company that generated the birth of the district.

In the wake of this success, the first spin-off products began to appear in the market. The barrier to entry was low. Despite requiring attention to detail, the process of sofa production was not particularly complex at that time. The production process consisted of only a few steps and, furthermore, there was wide availability of cheap labour.

In Matera, two partners of Natuzzi's decided to start their own businesses. These companies sensed the existence of a market with strong potential for expansion, that of leather upholstered furniture in the medium- and low-cost markets, and the subsequent development of design capabilities, production, commercial and distribution necessary to offer competitive products.

The three leading companies in the district – Natuzzi, Calia, and Nicoletti – stimulated the success of many subcontractors and, in some cases, encouraged employees to create their own businesses.

But it was with the listing of Natuzzi on the New York Stock Exchange that the big boom began in the area. The macroeconomic context was vibrant and, under the positive influence of Natuzzi, other manufacturers appeared. Companies specialized in the production of components of the finished product: wooden drums, polyurethane foam, padding, fabric and leather. Some companies decided, instead, to focus on a cheaper product, differentiating their offerings with a line of fabric sofas.

The whole district was involved in this period of growth. No longer limited to its original triangle, it began to extend to neighbouring areas such as Montescaglioso, Ferrandina, Pisticci, Gravina in Apulia, Cassano delle Murge, Laterza and Ginosa. This resulted in an intricate network of companies that were working, directly or indirectly, in exporting the Apulian dream.

Economic studies distinguish three types of companies in the composition of an industrial district:

- Leading enterprises
- Companies under contract
- Subcontractors

Leading enterprises have developed a system of relations with the market and are able to translate customer demands into production orders. These are companies governing the supply chain by controlling two basic stages of the value chain: product development and the relationship with the end customer.

Companies under contract are engaged in one or more stages of upholstered furniture production. These are highly specialized firms that receive support from the enterprise and generally also the raw material and semi-finished products. Their relationship with the leading company is through contract work.

Subcontractors are companies involved in the production of, for example, wooden casks, polyurethane, pins, bedsprings and mechanisms.

According to the Italian Minister of Economic Development,[26] the leading companies in the Apulia District were Natuzzi, Calia, Incanto, Nicoletti and Sofaland. All others were classified between the second and third categories mentioned above.

---

26 Ministero dello Sviluppo Economico (2012), Distretto del mobile imbottito della Murgia, document available at
     http://www.sviluppoeconomico.gov.it/index.php/it/incentivi/impresa/murge-distretto-del-mobile-imbottito

The competitiveness of industrial districts comes from four critical success factors:

- The breakdown (spatial and temporal) of the production cycle in the phases of manufacturing and specialization in the execution of each stage of production ensure cost competitiveness, high levels of flexibility and capacity for innovation;
- The specialization of production phases allows the achievement of economies of scale and learning that reduce unit costs and promote increased productivity;
- The distribution of production capacity among the various companies guarantees greater flexibility and the ability to quickly change the volume and quality of production and research in the district's appropriate production capacities;
- The geographical and productive proximity allows for the creation and transmission of knowledge and innovation.

It was indeed the merits of Natuzzi that contributed to the growth of the whole Murgia district during those years.

Natuzzi model 649, 1989

A processing phase in the Natuzzi Group tannery (Natco)

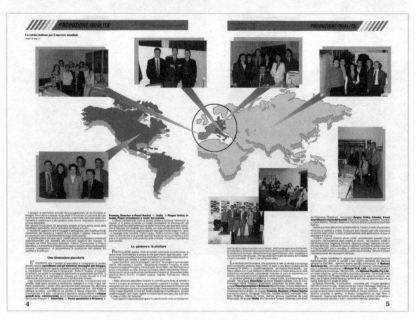

Natuzzi Commercial Organization in 1993

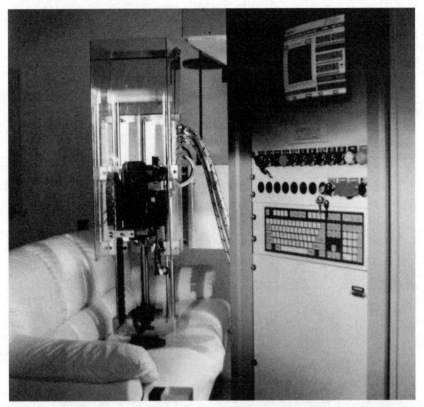

The natuzzi Quality Laboratory, Santeramo in Colle, 1996

A Divani&Divani shop in Italy, 1995

CHAPTER 5
THE YEARS OF TAKE-OFF
(1993-2000)

"I started thinking of trading on Wall Street in the United States around ten years ago – in the 1980s – when Natuzzi was growing and heavily exposed to the US market, and I understood there was really a possibility to create a big company ... The decision to open the doors of Industrie Natuzzi to external shareholdings was taken precisely with a view to create additional guarantees of stability for the future. Thanks to all of you, Natuzzi is today listed on the biggest stock market in the world, has the trust of thousands of investors and has excellent growth prospects ahead. Thanks to all of you, my friends."[27]

On Thursday, 13 May 1993 at around 8am, a delegation of managers led by Pasquale raced down Fifth Avenue in New York City by car. The shops were still closed.

The entrance of the New York Stock Exchange (NYSE) building was massive and conveyed a sense of solemnity.

Mr William H. Donaldson, chairman of the NYSE, welcomed the Natuzzi delegation for a business breakfast. There was silence in the room. The moment was magic for the delegation, full of dreams and determination, but also very aware of their history.

But this was not a normal business breakfast: after receiving his listing certificate, Pasquale closed his speech with the following words: *"The only thing I regret is that this wonderful room, in New York, is not big enough to host our 1,700 people who work in the company every day. It is to them that I extend my thanks: without their commitment, work and cooperation, we would not be here."*

After the business breakfast, the countdown began. Pasquale, his daughters Nunzia and Anna and the rest of the delegation descended into the trading enclosure. At 9.30am the bell rang, Industrie Natuzzi stock was called and Pasquale bought his first symbolic 100 stocks. It was done. All screens showed NTZ 15½, which meant the stock opened at the maximum expected level, 15.5 dollars.

---

27   Pasquale Natuzzi in Crescere Insieme, 1993, vol. 6, page 1.

Just to give you an idea, only 13 Italian companies were listed on the NYSE at that time, and Natuzzi was one of them.

Without any doubt, the listing was a great opportunity for Natuzzi to access the finance market at a lower price than local banks in Apulia, but it was also a great chance for the company to improve its overall structure.

It was the result of the incredible dedication of men and women and resources that made something unimaginable on paper a reality: a family-owned business, from the south of Italy, listed on the NYSE.

Giuseppe Desantis, Vice Chairman and COO at that time, recalled the period with these words.

"We were working 24-7, during the day on regular business and in the evening trying to deal with the enormous quantity of requests the American lawyers had made of us. I look back at that period as a fascinating one. During the road show we were visiting five states a day and we had to convince investors, sometimes sleepy, as the meetings started at 7am, to buy our stock in 20 minutes.

"We had few documents and a very practical approach. Our sales pitch was the solidity of the company, the international exposure, the social mission, the transparency of the company and the brand awareness. To give you an idea of how famous Mr Pasquale Natuzzi was in the United States, it was not so uncommon that at the immigration offices in the US airport agents used to say, "Ah, Mr Natuzzi, you are the one."

"That we did all this in such a short time is quite incredible. This shows the great ability of a leader such as Pasquale Natuzzi to create a vision and push the whole team towards that direction.

"I still remember the Italian newspapers started to really acknowledge Natuzzi after the listing on NYSE."[28]

The listing represented a time to take stock of the growth of the previous years and plan the future. *"From scratch, we created an entrepreneurial culture around upholstered furniture in the south of Italy and around*

50 companies are now involved in the production, establishing what is called the Triangle of Upholstered Furniture and creating jobs indirectly for more than 1,000 people," said Pasquale.[29]

Last, but not least, the listing for Natuzzi was seen as a way to redeem the Italian reputation worldwide. It revealed that Southern Italy was not just a place of scandals, mafia and negative images sometimes depicted by newspapers, but it was also a place where courage, resilience and hard work were rewarded and recognized. In a video used during the road show in the US, the company affirmed, *"Loving our work has made us the leading craftsmen in the world."*

The first shareholders were the Salomon Brothers, Prudential Securities, Goldman Sachs and Credit Lyonnais. This created a big responsibility for the management of Natuzzi, but also an inspiring challenge.

The listing marked a period of prosperity and the start of a continuing evolution for Natuzzi.

---

28   Giuseppe Desantis, interview performed in January 2017.
29   Crescere Insieme n. 6/1993, page 1.

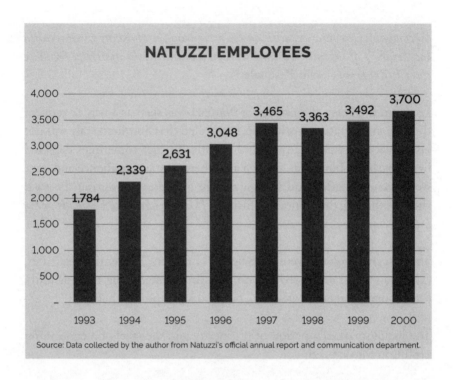

NATUZZI EMPLOYEES

Source: Data collected by the author from Natuzzi's official annual report and communication department.

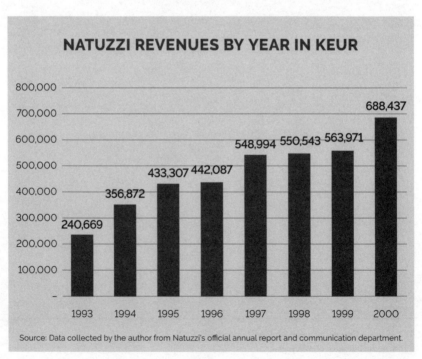

NATUZZI REVENUES BY YEAR IN KEUR

Source: Data collected by the author from Natuzzi's official annual report and communication department.

The workforce increased to 3,700 people in 2000, revenue increased year on year, reaching 688 million euros and the number of seats produced was around 2,600 million.

This growth generated a high level of complexity in the company, driven by the deep customization of products, reflected in organizational and commercial topics.

This was sustained by different elements: a company reorganization, a focus on human resources, Pasquale's willingness to keep the link with his employees, strengthening Natuzzi's management style and continuous focus on the customer.

The Company Reorganization

The company reorganization was initiated to ensure a shared decisional process and a structured functional organization. This evolution allowed a more professional management of the different areas of the company, but also freed up the founder and gave him the opportunity to keep his attention on the big picture.

The company tried to align employee and manager behaviours through clarifying expectations and sharing key principles.

Focusing on management behaviours, Giuseppe Desantis, vice chairman, recalled the following:[30]

- **Results first**: to achieve results, we needed always to be the problem solver. Attitudes of resignation and surrender only generated distrust, frustration and inefficiencies. We had to learn to work with optimism and enthusiasm, together with the right mix of determination and wilfulness.
- **Words fly, results remain**: each one of us must create tangible results, not bureaucracy, operating solutions and not a list of problems. If something went wrong in the company, it could have generated

---

30   Crescere Insieme vol. 28/98, page 14.

additional costs, waste and poor quality, which means an unhappy customer. Losing customers threatened the economic stability of the company and jeopardized jobs.

- **Communicate, always**: communication skills were fundamental to working well. To get better results, we needed to go over formal rules and talk with the key stakeholders, especially those in authority, particularly if we had already shared with our manager and they have not listened to us. If a problem existed, it must be solved, regardless of hierarchy.

- **Fair play, please**: mutual respect and courtesy were key in all departments. Sometimes we had a hard time achieving results because of the wilful obtuseness of some people.

- **I am the protagonist of my work**: we should all feel as though we were the protagonists of our work. Not merely doers, we must work as entrepreneurs and not just employees; we needed to invest, research, create and promote new ways of working to improve our activities. Pave the way and obtain results that make yourself proud and instill in others a spirit of emulation, opening the way to further career opportunities.

The Focus on Human Resources

The attention to people and human resources was another key enabler at the core of Natuzzi's growth strategy.

To motivate all employees and increase their performance, a new corporate incentive system was introduced at the beginning of the 1990s. The system was based on a variable performance appraisal that was calculated on a monthly basis, according to efficiency, productivity and quality parameters and was paid to employees every six months. It involved the whole workforce and endeavoured to create a more direct involvement of people in the company's financial results.

A stock option incentive plan was also launched some years later, in 1994. In line with Pasquale's beliefs, it was extended to 255 employees selected by criteria such as their role in the company (i.e., head of department, head of a unit) and years served (more than ten). This demonstrated the belief that experience, dedication and accountability were rewarded in Natuzzi, regardless of academic prowess or level within the organization.

A full mapping of job positions and competencies was prepared to organize internal education and establish a more professional recruitment process. To share Natuzzi's principles and motivate new employees to become a member of the family, each was given a copy of the annual report and the latest issue of the in-house magazine by Michele Bonerba, the director of human resources and organization.

Joining Natuzzi in these years was like *"winning a competition,"* said one employee. *"I joined Natuzzi not because of money, but because it represented a quantum leap. I knew from my friends working there the high level of attention the company paid to its resources at all levels,"* recalled Mario Di Santo. [31]

A thorough initiation for all newcomers, whatever their department or position, helped them feel like they were not just a number but a key part of the workforce. By helping them fully understand the organization, the company was able to unlock their potential to contribute to the success of the team in which they would be working.

A set of introductory courses was created in 1996, with the aim of motivating the internal craftsmen and speeding up the learning curve of new employees. [32]

Pasquale strongly believed that individual productivity was key to growth.

The company continued to put education at its core and founded the Natuzzi Professional Training School in 1997 to coordinate and deliver training modules to all employees.

Under the management of Michele Bonerba, this structure became even more advanced, involving people from outside the company. A set of

---

31   Di Santo Mario, interview performed in January 2017.
32   Crescere Insieme, vol.4 /1992, page 6.

courses was set up targeting young people, to educate them and create a potential pool of new candidates.

"The future belongs to those with capability rather than a job. Those who simply hold a job will sooner or later become a luxury for a company, while those with strong capabilities, with a love for their work and talent, will be key for any organization. After attending courses at Natuzzi Corporate University, some people will stay with us, others will go to work for our competitors, but they all will have in common one thing that we will have given them: a love for their work."[33]

These combined efforts led to Natuzzi winning the Sinergia Award[34] in 1998 from the Italian Association of Human Resources Directors. This honour was based on *"the central key role human resources have had and still have in the company and the development put in place from the company human resource department to move from a family company to a managerial one through advanced management procedures."*[35]

Strengthening Natuzzi's Management Style While Keeping the Link with All Employees

In 1999, Pasquale highlighted the importance of company management to move on from the 'good old times' and become leaders, combining all efforts towards product, creativity, price and service. These were the key success factors that allowed the company to maintain the competitive advantage it had created for itself over the past years.

The managerial style of Natuzzi's employees was articulated in ten golden rules:

1. Respect for people
2. 'Participate and delegate' attitude
3. Listening and communication skills

---

33 Pasquale Natuzzi in Crescere Insieme, vol.21 /1997, page 3.

34 The Sinergia Award is an Italian prestigious recognition of the Italian Association of Human Resources Directors aimed at recognizing the value of the best human resources management program across companies.

35 Crescere Insieme, vol.32/98, page 12.

4. Fairness, correctness and consistency
5. Sense of belonging to the team
6. Walk the talk
7. Sharing ideas
8. Problem-solving attitude
9. Act locally, think globally
10. Standing on company decisions

Within the first pages of a booklet dedicated to new employees was a note from Pasquale, which read, *"Some years ago, it was a great pleasure and matter of pride for me to introduce myself to each single new employee, shake their hand and then wish them good luck. However, this is now no longer possible. And this is, believe me, my only regret, though inevitable, due to our extraordinary growth over the past years. We really are a lot of people today!"*

The document also contained Natuzzi's ten commandments:

1. The customer is our most important asset
2. We put our love in our job
3. Quality of product is the quality of our employees
4. Simplify the complexity
5. Knowledge is the foundation of each solution
6. Communication exchange is key to growth
7. I work, I create work
8. Value of the family
9. Always improve
10. Think about the future

A key component of the management style was the lack of hierarchies.

A strong way to connect with employees was the annual Christmas party. At Natuzzi, they chose this yearly celebration to share results and celebrate successes. These events were chronicled in the in-house magazine and the company video library. Christmas parties were opportunities to get together and share the founder's vision on the company's overall direction in an open and direct way with all employees.

One employee recalled those corporate events with the following words: *"They were really a party! I still remember my girlfriend and our friends queuing at the hairdresser in the afternoon in order to look beautiful for the occasion. Going around the party you could smell the happiness, you could see smiles and could feel proud for what you were part of. Even people outside of Natuzzi knew about the event, since the whole community looked forward to them with huge curiosity,"* said Mario Di Santo.[36]

Others added: *"Corporate party attendants can be split into two main groups: those who want to participate and those who feel they have to be there, because of the role they have, because of their managers, etc. At Natuzzi's Christmas party, there was a climate of total participation. I still remember, in 1993, when Pasquale Natuzzi started his speech, there was a standing ovation with the same level of energy you could see at a rock concert. You didn't feel the distance between you and him, but you could feel the willingness to grow together, to improve, to generate positive results and then to celebrate the success on Christmas. The dedication was total and you could see it in people's eyes,"* said Gianmichele Pace.[37]

"It was a party: the speech from the president and then a concert, live music, karaoke. The company was looking beautiful, and you had to look beautiful, too. You were part of that beauty, since your work was directly creating it. The atmosphere was simply fantastic!" recalled Gianni Romaniello.[38]

The recurring messages during each celebration were trust, loyalty to the company, collaboration and family.

"At Natuzzi, our highly specialized people have grown to consider the company part of their family and 90% of our managers have been promoted from within. All these are a rare and precious heritage that we must protect" – said Pasquale.[39]

This approach to people and the recognition of their talents, their support and their dedication to work was also reflected in the low turnover of the company and the absence of employee strikes. These positive emotions continued. *"We have created a great company, we have created a solid company, we have created a strong company and I have to thank all those who have helped me carry on this wonderful mission,"* said Pasquale.

"I am in love with this company. After 36 years working in this company, in the morning I wake up with an enthusiasm and an incredible energy. We must continue to help our territory."[40]

During the 1995 Christmas party, after Pasquale's speech, a banner appeared with the words 'WE LOVE THE PRESIDENT!'. The devotion of employees was so strong that some employees also wrote a song about Natuzzi, the words of which are particularly interesting:

*"Thirty years ago in Santeramo
people lived only with agriculture,
some crazy ones jumped on the train
and went abroad looking for luck.
... And then there was the small army:
that of the masons,
who worked 13 hours per day
to enrich certain manufacturers.
Thank God suddenly
Natuzzi industry arrived
and in no time, in Santeramo in Murgia,
almost everything changed.*

*In the largest desert of Southern Italy,
Industria Natuzzi is like an oasis
Almost all politicians of Southern Italy
They are just watching
but they all envy us."*

You can read through the lines the perception of Natuzzi's employees about their company: a way to give dignity back to the people of Apulia by encouraging those who emigrated looking for a job to come back to their origins.

---

36   Mario Di Santo, interview performed in January 2017.

37   Gianmichele Pace, interview performed in January 2017.

38   Gianni Romaniello, interview performed in January 2017.

39   Crescere Insieme, vol 10/1994, page 7.

40   Pasquale Natuzzi, Christmas party speech, 1995. Quote from a company video.

Even in this big, structured company, with more than 3,000 employees, it was evident how the leader and founder had the ability to create a common view and energize the people through his words.

In 1996, a new motto was launched: 'Natuzzi quality people', to portray the link between quality of life, quality of work and quality of people. And some may say the founder still behaved like a father from the south of Italy, but it was indeed this capacity to be clear, direct and down-to-earth that made him a strong leader over these years. He was a self-made man with a clear vision.

The strong conviction at Natuzzi in these years was about *"working better to live better: quality of the work to improve quality of life"*.[41] This was then translated in all aspects of internal training organized by the human resources department. Nunzia Natuzzi, in 1996, declared, *"Our company must continue to be the engine not only of economic, but also cultural development, in all the territories in which there are companies of the Group."*[42]

Collaborations with Italian universities were activated, offering scholarships and sharing the business knowledge acquired through active participation in lessons and workshops.

During these years, Natuzzi positioned itself in a quite different way from its competitors in Apulia: *"In a world marked by high unemployment and small businesses that pay little money and are in the black, Natuzzi offers a stable job to a growing number of young people."*[43]

Working at Natuzzi continued to be a privilege, as many in the area struggled to find work and were often underpaid, partly as a result of the strong expansion of the upholstered furniture industry.

Being able to work in a factory with a regular salary represented a real revolution for Annunziata Marino, a young employee hired by the company in 1976: *"I was 18 years old when I joined the company. Before that, working meant sewing clothes in a small workshop in the village, where they paid you once in a while, 40,000 or 50,000 lire. The impact was very strong. Now working and living together with 50 other people in a manufacturing plantthat seemed huge, being paid regularly every month, taking a salary of 180,000 lire; this for me was a real revolution."*[44]

Employees started talking about 'The Natuzzi Miracle'. In those years, no conflicts, low unionization, high employee participation in the company's fortunes and choices, identification with the leader and effective vertical communication were the typical characteristics of the company.

The Importance of Orchestrating Internal Processes

Although the holistic focus on human resources was indeed a key lever to sustain the extensive growth of these years, a strong focus on the market and on internal processes was also evident.

In these years, Natuzzi got its first ISO 9000 quality certification, which is the international standard of quality management and quality assurance. This was an important step for Natuzzi, but also for the whole industry, as many other companies started following suit.

Quality inspectors were established to check all stages of production in all sites, building a wide database of statistics useful for future production. Quality soon came to be considered the glue that kept all the departments together.

In 1995, a suggestion box system was created: every employee at every level could contribute to the increased performance of the company by highlighting areas that needed improvement. The employees whose suggestions were implemented were financially rewarded or received special prizes.

---

41   Crescere Insieme, vol 12/1995, page 8.
42   Crescere Insieme, vol 16/1996, page 4.
43   Sinisi A., "Natuzzi. Un divano a Wall Street," Egea, 2008.
44   Pianeta Natuzzi n. 0/1991.

In 1996, Pasquale Natuzzi was presented with the Italian Quality Award[45] by the president of the Italian Republic, Oscar Luigi Scalfaro. Awarded by the Leonardo Committee (a group of entrepreneurs, artists, scientists, and men and women of culture), this award recognized business quality and excellence criteria and encouraged Italian businesses to become more competitive in the world economy.

Winners are those considered to best represent the image of Italy to the world and that have achieved great success in international markets. In the past, this award has been given to Leonardo del Vecchio, Sergio and Luigi Loro Piana, Luciano Benetton and Miuccia Prada.

In 1997, an internal quality challenge was launched: the idea being to assess the best production sites on a monthly and annual basis through a quality index (based on internal inspections). The motto for which is quite charming: *The quality of my job creates jobs!*

To encourage a reduction in employee absences, a healthy competition across different production plants was established, with individual and team contributions to the overall target of productivity of the company. This effort succeeded in reducing the absence ratio to 2.35% in 1997, down from 3.36% in 1993.

---

45   Translation of 'Premio Qualità Italia'.

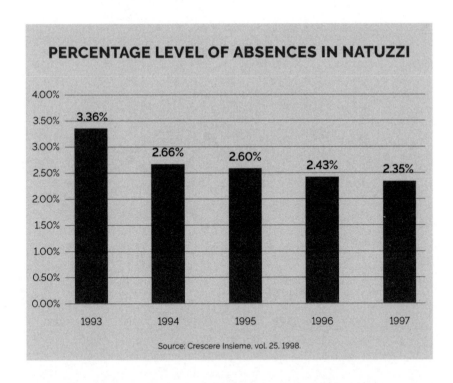

PERCENTAGE LEVEL OF ABSENCES IN NATUZZI

Source: Crescere Insieme, vol. 25, 1998.

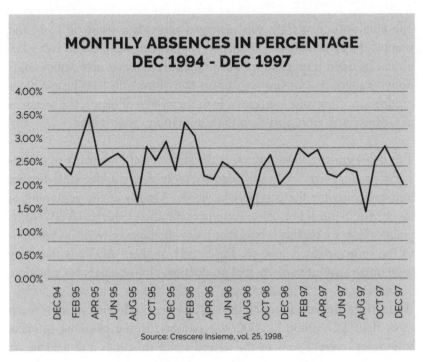

MONTHLY ABSENCES IN PERCENTAGE
DEC 1994 - DEC 1997

Source: Crescere Insieme, vol. 25, 1998.

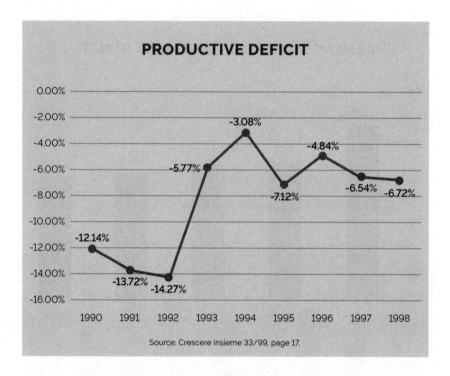

PRODUCTIVE DEFICIT

Source: Crescere insieme 33/99, page 17.

The attention on margin was managed through a focus on costs and vendors. In particular, the production engineering department was a key player. Its main responsibility was to identify, develop and deploy solutions to support company expansion and allow effective 'just-in-time' production. They were concerned with the design of plants, the selection of facilities and tools, and even the automation systems used.

This department also kept track of the statistics of each plant, to understand productivity levels and identify tools that could enable further improvements for the company as whole. Already at the beginning of the 1990s, Natuzzi was using Automatic Guided Vehicles (AGV) in its plants; these are mobile robots that follow markers or wires on the floor to transport products around. The beauty of these AGVs is that they were integrated into an artisanal production, almost a paradox situation.

An increase and rapid growth in sales saw the production of sofas reach more than 2.5 million in 2000; this required strong planning to make sure orders were closed in the agreed-upon timelines and a focus on transportation and logistics to deliver the goods to customers on time. Due to high customer demands, there was a period where the delivery time increased from six to 18 weeks. Thanks to the extraordinary efforts of the employees, the orders got back on track and the average delivery period was reduced back to eight weeks.

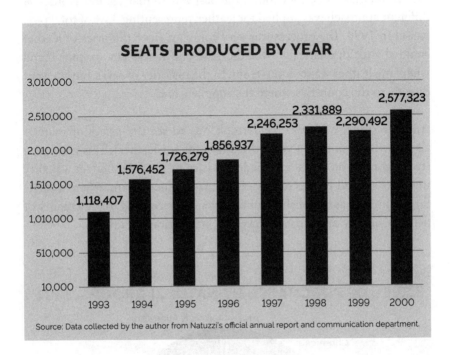

SEATS PRODUCED BY YEAR

Source: Data collected by the author from Natuzzi's official annual report and communication department.

To reduce the delivery time in Natuzzi's key market, the US, the 'Quick Ship Program' was introduced. This was a special agreement with Natuzzi's main US customers, in which a limited number of models (30 models in 30 colours) would be produced and sold to each customer. This program successfully reduced the time to market on the East Coast to five weeks and on the West Coast to seven weeks.

To optimize distribution channels in Italy, Natuzzi builds G.A.R.A. (the Associated Group of Furniture resellers). This specialized buying group aimed to combine the needs of small shops and provide one single interface for the market. The buyers at G.A.R.A. purchased Natuzzi products at the best price available on behalf of small local dealers.

A single supply chain department was set up for all companies of the group and benefited Natuzzi in terms of economies of scale, but also large quantities and more bargaining power with vendors. Even in this part of the company, you could see the Taylorism approach: every buyer was specialized in one type of product and, through this specialization, they could make sure they found the best way to manage every order. A different approach was applied for leather, representing 43% of total purchases in 1994. The process was very complex, since the price of leather could change dramatically over the year, and it was key to understand where the leather was coming from. In the majority of cases, buyers went directly to the countries where the suppliers are.

Another strategy Natuzzi undertook was to set the prices of materials over the period of a year (three months for leather). This ensured a strong control on costs and made it easier to plan the budget. Quality was next tackled by the supply chain management team, where a satisfaction index was established for each vendor according to punctuality of delivery, quality of goods and level of certification obtained.

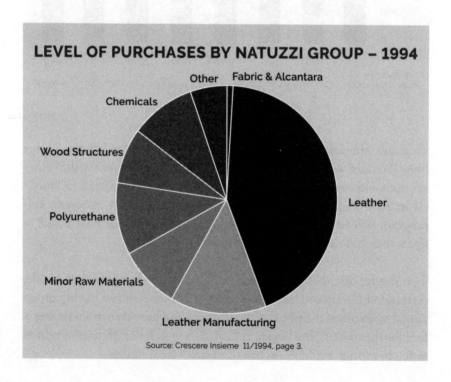

LEVEL OF PURCHASES BY NATUZZI GROUP – 1994

Other — Fabric & Alcantara — Chemicals — Wood Structures — Polyurethane — Minor Raw Materials — Leather Manufacturing — Leather

Source: Crescere Insieme 11/1994, page 3.

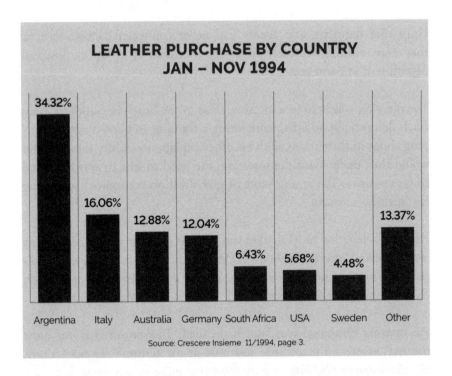

LEATHER PURCHASE BY COUNTRY
JAN – NOV 1994

- Argentina: 34.32%
- Italy: 16.06%
- Australia: 12.88%
- Germany: 12.04%
- South Africa: 6.43%
- USA: 5.68%
- Sweden: 4.48%
- Other: 13.37%

Source: Crescere Insieme 11/1994, page 3.

From a market standpoint, this period concentrated on expanding volumes in all market segments by developing direct channels of distribution.

Continuous Focus on the Customer

Pasquale paid a lot of attention to his ambassadors in the markets: Natuzzi's sale agents. The commercial network was reinforced over the years and, on top of the commercial company based in the US (Natuzzi Americas Inc.), Natuzzi UK, based in London, and Natuzzi Pacific Pty Let, based in Sydney, were created.

To further strengthen this network, Natuzzi held its first International Marketing Meeting for its 123 sale agents in 1997, a crucial year for the company, since it exceeded 1 billion ITL in net sales and delivered in one year the growth that had been planned for two (production +12%, sales +6% and net income +38%).

Until that moment, sale agents had never connected face-to-face, as they were working remotely under the coordination of the commercial department in Santeramo.

The meeting was held in a location close to the beach in Southern Italy. Each delegate found a bag containing a training suit and a pair of running shoes in their room, with no other explanation. Only the day after would they understand the meaning: the need to run, to stay agile and be competitive. The strong wave of globalization was quickly changing the business scenario.

Pasquale's devotion to its market was evident over the years. *"I exist if my customer exists,"* was a simple truth Pasquale believed in. *"We search for the full happiness and satisfaction of our customer and confirmation of his trust: the basic conditions for us to exist."*

An internal campaign was launched called 'The customer is our most precious asset' and placed the customer at the centre: *"The pearl is rare, like the customer. God help us if we think that winning a customer is an easy thing. The pearl is valuable, no less than a customer. The pearl is inside the shell, until someone takes it away. We try to represent, for all our pearls, the more protective, the best possible shell."*

Natuzzi's marketing department became massively important during these years. It took on the role of listening, reading and capturing market needs through a deep understanding of customer reasons for purchase, including customer preferences, lifestyles and also key drivers. It had to define sustainable targets, based on market growth, but also on company resources and capabilities.

Natuzzi's distinguishing product strategy was key in sustaining growth. This strategy was based on different categories of upholstered furniture in a variety of finishes (leather, fabric, microfiber, Alcantara[46]), in a variety of styles (modern, contemporary and traditional), with different functionality (gate and reclining sofas) and price ranges.[47]

A key success factor was the stylish Italian design of Natuzzi's products and, soon after, 'Natuzzi' became 'The Italian way to say sofa'.[48]

The ability to combine aesthetic quality with a wide range of colours and shapes, and new models every year, positioned Natuzzi *"one step ahead all the time in price, styling and quality."*[49] In order to stay in the game, many competitors began to imitate Natuzzi products. To avoid such imitations, the company offered 86 different models in 1986, and after only three years, its catalogue had around 230 products!

The extensive number of models produced by Natuzzi supported and improved relationships with customers and allowed the company to stay at the top of its sector. Natuzzi was in a position where it could offer customers exclusivity on a specific product/range, creating a win-win situation where customers/dealers would not be competing with each other, as they would have different Natuzzi products and ranges. At the same time, this provided Natuzzi with an extremely profitable way to enlarge its market coverage.

Part of the strategy was the acquisition of a well-known Italian company, Spagnesi SpA, for its upholstered furniture. The idea was to combine the commercial power of Natuzzi with the valuable expertise of Spagnesi to create a new line of sofas with wood trim.

The key was to continue Natuzzi's growth and balance the geographic footprint and product mix at the same time, to create a 'Natuzzi style' around all type of sofas.

Looking at the geographic landscape, the Americas were contributing 'only' 47.6% of group revenues in 1998 (compared with more than 90% in the early 1990s), while growth in Europe contributed to around 42% of the group revenues and the residual 10% came from the rest of the world (mainly Australia, Japan and the Middle East).

---

46   Alcantara is a covering material manufactured and marketed by Alcantara SpA. It is primarily used in the design, fashion, accessories, consumer electronics, automotive and marine industries

47   Sinisi A., "Natuzzi. Un divano a Wall Street," Egea, 2008.

48   Ibid.

49   ibid.

The experience in Italy, started some years earlier with the experiment of the Divani&Divani chain, was proceeding quite well.

Nicola Masotina was the director of the project at that time. *"When I joined Natuzzi, I refined the internal organization of the franchising department to increase the speed of opening new shops and meanwhile develop services to affiliates to ensure a proper management of shops. The response from my colleagues was exceptional: we all rolled up our sleeves and, in December 1994, we opened 32 shops, an average of one shop every ten days!"*[50] he said.

The number of shops continued to grow in all regions of Italy. This was a revolution in the market since, with the exception of Ikea, this had not yet applied in the furniture industry and no other producer was adopting this franchising formula at the time. The decision was based on the fact that the upholstered furniture market in Italy was one of the richest in Europe and, through the franchising formula, Natuzzi could fully control the distribution: from local marketing campaigns to training sellers and supporting local shops.

The local press referred to this phenomenon as *"an example of modernization"*: for the first time in Italy, people could sit on the sofa, try it without any plastic protection and then decide to buy it.

"I remember furniture shops were sceptical initially, but today I am very proud of the Divani&Divani adventure. It has been an exciting experience, the first experiment of a franchising formula applied to the furniture market in Italy.

"During that time, we got an extremely high number of requests to become franchisees. We created a cash machine: some of them were able to recover the investment in only six months. There was nothing similar in the market and the approach chosen by the company was also innovative.

"One day, Pasquale Natuzzi called us in his office and said, 'Now you have to convince me to open a Divani&Divani shop.'

"We explained the different reasons to do so, the rationale behind it and, at the end of our speech, he said, 'Okay, good. From now on you have to work for the

interests of the franchisee, because if you work for their interests, you work for my interest,"[51] Gianmichele Pace said.

The basic idea was really to create a partnership with the shops to promote and sustain the products in the market. To be closer to the market and follow the new trends in the late 1990s, the website www.natuzzi. com was also created.

The Rise of the Murgia District

During these years, the district had a strong concentration of micro and small enterprises, which represented nearly 80% of the companies in the district. The entire district of Matera and Santeramo was divided between 'good jobs', mostly in large, well-structured companies and 'bad jobs' in companies working as subcontractors.

Small companies in the sector tended to have a workforce of mainly women of a young age (average of 22–24 years) with a low level of education (90% elementary school).[52]

Looking at the volumes generated, excluding the leading companies, 3% had an annual turnover of less than €75,000, 15% had between €76,000 and 250,000, 9% between €251,000 and 500,000, 21% up to 1 million euro, 31% had a turnover up to 1 million euro and finally, 21% over 5 million euro. This means that although the size was small, these companies were able to generate high volumes of sales.

At the peak of its development, the district had 14,000 employees and around 500 companies involved, directly or indirectly, in sofa production. This district produced 55% of Italian upholstery products and 16% of the world's.

---

50   Crescere Insieme, 21/97, page 5.

51   Gianmichele Pace, interview performed in January 2017.

52   Sinisi A., "Natuzzi. Un divano a Wall Street," Egea, 2008.

What distinguished the development and success of these districts in Italy was the spontaneity of the initiatives promoted by the entrepreneurs. Over the years, these entrepreneurs developed specialized expertise in certain sectors and grew their companies based on informal relationships with other companies within the territory.[53] The spontaneity that characterized the densification process of the districts and the natural way with which connections were established among companies operating in a certain area, rules out the possibility of replicating this in other areas. Empirical research confirms this.

The strong focus on quality and attention to detail was transferred to the whole district, creating a virtuous mechanism of growth. Leading companies also helped educate on issues such as quality certification, legality and respect for the environment.

This was the era of industrialization of the production: just-in-time techniques, together with new production and organization approaches, definition of standard minutes to create a model and standardization of certain components (i.e., frame and stuffing). The attention to design and the launch of a new collection every year helped penetrate the market and generate high volumes.

The Districts and Economic Theory

From an economic theory standpoint, firms located in the districts take on different characteristics based on variables such as the strategic autonomy and the degree of stability of the companies.

By combining these two variables, there is another interesting model used to study a district, proposed by Italian economist Ricciardi in 2013.

---

53   Ricciardi A., I distretti industriali italiani:recenti tendenze evolutive, Sinergie, 2013, n. 91, pp. 21-58.

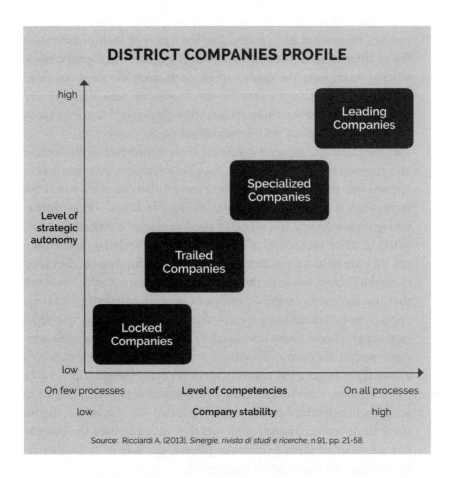

Source: Ricciardi A. (2013), *Sinergie, rivista di studi e ricerche*, n.91, pp. 21-58.

Based on the variables, we can identify four profiles of district companies:

- The locked companies are small or very small (workshops) special-izing in single processing steps and low professional content. They are able to guarantee low costs and adequate quality standards, but unable to express autonomy in strategic choices appropriate to insert independently in the market. Weak from a contractual standpoint, these companies are closely dependent on customers of other busi-nesses and are suffering the effects of the crisis by recording the high-est rates of closures and bankruptcies;
- The trailed companies oversee the critical functions of production, including through the network of local suppliers, but as businesses blocked assume an adaptive-imitative behaviour especially towards

product innovation and process. For the limits of their organization fail to directly seize the opportunities of growth and exports, while striving to improve the quality of products, basically their competitive strategy is resolved to exploit the conditions offered by the district context, but when these are less strongly exposed to competition from foreign suppliers with lower labour costs;

- The specialized companies focus on high production skills (design and engineering of the product), are able to achieve, even using specialized sub-suppliers, semi-finished and finished products with high technological content, but hardly under its own brand. These companies generally have a few stages of production, are development-oriented in their technological innovations and exclusive know-how, but they are weak on the commercial level. For this reason, they tend to establish close ties with the contracting companies, with the result that the autonomy in the formulation of their competitive strategy appears to be conditioned by the third parties, together with their own brands. These companies tend to occupy a more profitable segment within the sector. They have a higher barrier to entry, which allows them to get away from competition from foreign suppliers. In some districts, the most dynamic, specialized companies, thanks to a higher international profile, have expanded the number of clients, particularly multinational companies that have favoured the innovative activities of these enterprises playing the role of technological knowledge and transmitters managerial;

- Some district top-level companies, not necessarily larger than the others, but more structured, appear. These are typically present at end-markets, including international ones, with technological knowledge and have more contractual power. They often have established brands both nationally and internationally, with strong autonomy in drawing up decisions on the end-markets, they are able to perform all stages of the production process internally, with expertise in R&D and sales. In essence, they act as forces that drive local development and play an important role as intermediary between the market and the local system.

All these four categories of companies could be found in the Murgia district.

The New Show Room in High Point and the Rise in Pasquale's Worldwide Reputation

Another key milestone during these years of take-off was the opening of the new US office and showroom.

Having been the initial key market for Natuzzi, the US was still close to Pasquale's heart. And when the right opportunity came, Pasquale decided to invest $6 million and buy a new venue for the US office, Natuzzi Upholstery Inc. He bought 100,000 square metres of land, previously occupied by a hotel in High Point, North Carolina.

The project came to the attention of well-known, award-winning Italian architect Mario Bellini. He has 25 pieces in the permanent design collection of the Museum of Modern Art (MoMA) in New York. Among the buildings he has designed are the Portello Trade Fair District in Milan, the Villa Erba Exhibition and Convention Centre in Cernobbio (Como, Italy), the Tokyo Design Centre in Japan, the National Gallery of Victoria in Melbourne (Australia), the Deutsche Bank Headquarters in Frankfurt (Germany), the City History Museum of Bologna (Italy), the Department of Islamic Art at the Louvre in Paris (France) and the new Milan Convention Centre (Italy). And, obviously, the Natuzzi America Headquarters in the US, a choice driven by beauty and elegance of the Italian style.

The whole building was 10,000 square metres, 4,000 square metres of which were dedicated to the showroom. The construction began in September 1996 and the opening was planned for June 1998. Pasquale was enthusiastic, saying, *"We will astonish our customers, showing them the largest assortment of upholstered furniture in the world."*[54]

The preparation took two full years, during which a dedicated task force was put in place in Santeramo, with prototypists, designers and R&D. The idea was to create a new collection for the great opening and Pasquale knew that he wanted to be involved in the front lines. He moved his office inside the 'idea factory', an area within Natuzzi headquarters

---

54   Crescere Insieme, vol. 25, March 1998, page 3.

where they were writing the future of the company. He decided that, *"All meetings of the executive committee should be held here, so the vital energy of this season is then spread around all the company."*

This was also an opportunity to put together three strategic departments: R&D, costings and prototypes. The idea was to create a 'factory within the factory', where the whole creative process was run in a holistic way, from choosing materials to designing shapes, building prototypes and estimating costs of production.

On 23 April 1998, outside 139 West Commerce Avenue in High Point, the blue ribbon was cut and Natuzzi's ship set sail!

The day started at 7.30am in the meeting room on the fourth floor. Pasquale and Jeff Baron (director and president of Natuzzi Americas) gathered managers and agents to review the order signed during the High Point Interior Design Fair the day before: a strong sign of the founder's pragmatism. During the day, clients were welcomed by the agents and guided through more than 260 models; they were transformed from general observers into careful reviewers of every model on display. In the afternoon, the official celebration was conducted in the presence of the mayor of High Point, Rebecca Smothers, the town's parish priest, Father Philip Kollithanath, and around 200 people.

"I am honoured to celebrate, with you, our new showroom inauguration. This building was designed by noted Italian architect Mario Bellini, who represents the highest expression of Italian creativity. I appreciate very much his distinctive simplicity," said Pasquale Natuzzi.

"The shape of the building evokes a ship because crossing the Atlantic gave me the chance to come here, enter your wonderful country and enjoy its exciting opportunities. The bow represents our natural attitude to look forward. The cross-section of the building, with its glass windows along Elm Street, symbolizes our way of being always transparent.

"So, I am very proud of this innovative structure, which is also a tribute dedicated to the wonderful people of High Point. Thank you so much for your warm hospitality and welcome to the World of Natuzzi."

The atmosphere was warm and welcoming, with music and smiling and curious faces all around.

"I was here six months ago and I can't believe that you have achieved all this in such a short time. I didn't think it was possible," Karl Kunkel, editor of *Triad Business News*, stated.[55]

Word spread around town and, two hours after the opening ceremony, the number of guests had grown to 2,000!

"From this moment onward, whoever comes to High Point will not be able to do so without a visit to Natuzzi," said Eklain England, vice chairman of Elmo America.

To mark the occasion, British customer Uno, a retail chain with 49 shops in the UK, sent 240 splendid roses with a small note: *"To all industry Natuzzi. One rose for each shop of our supplier of choice. Wish we were there to share your success. From your absent friends in the UK."* This shows again the market orientation of Natuzzi and its relationship with its dealers.

The High Point building became a reference point for anyone walking in the city.

However, all this fame and market recognition was not reflected by the media until the mid-90s, when Natuzzi celebrated 35 years of activity. At this time, Pasquale was still as involved in the company as he had been in the beginning, and this prompted the press to take an interest in his personality and the miracle of his company.

Forbes[56] referred to him as "a methodical man" and in 1997 posed the question: *"How did a man from an area so remote build a business that ships to the four corners of the world?"*

The answer given in *Forbes* was, *"In part, by accident."*

---

55 Crescere Insieme, vol. 27, May/June 1998.

"In the 1970s and 1980s, when he was struggling to build his business by making leather furniture an affordable middle-class purchase, many small Italian stores wanted to buy sofas from him, but only if he would help them avoid Italy's crushing taxes. 'They ask for three sofas, but invoice for just one or two,' he says. 'Everyone was trying to be smart. But if the taxman came, I would be the one in trouble.'"

So, he had to focus on looking for clients overseas and, in 1982, he went to New York and sold 100 sofas to Macy's for $445 each. Macy's sold them at retail for $999.

During this time, Pasquale started to realize that Natuzzi was operating like a fashion business. Each year they were adding 125 new models, each available in 250 different leathers. Overall, the variety of combinations meant they were offering more than a million products to their customers. These included products made using regulation fire-retardant foam for Californians, to the harder seats preferred by Germans.

Businessweek referred to him and his company as *"an undiscovered Italian gem"*.[57]

Natuzzi was certainly an example of an 'undiscovered gem' in the global market, and had the potential of becoming a blue-chip company, say Raphael and Lerner, co-managers of the First Eagle International Fund.

"Certainly, we expect Natuzzi's stock to become as hot as its leather sofas," says Raphael.

"Natuzzi is unrivalled in the furniture industry for high-quality products, manufacturing automation and employee loyalty."

Peter Fuhrman, in *Forbes*, refers to Pasquale as being different to *"your average Italian industrialist. He has a shaved head and wears floral shirts so loud they're almost deafening. He appears in most of the company's trade advertising looking a little like Mr Clean in a Versace outfit. But beneath this somewhat surreal image is a very sober and disciplined businessman."*[58]

Maureen Kline, in *The Wall Street Journal*, referred to Pasquale as, *"A rare case of a person where creativity and common sense are in perfect balance."*[59]

Kathleen M. Berry pointed out how the success of Natuzzi was thanks to *"a management information system that ties every order for a sofa or loveseat to automated production. It has invested heavily in technologies and produces its own materials because suppliers were unable to meet its demands."*[60]

Lisa Bannon[61] from *The Wall Street Journal* wrote that, *"Bucking the stereotype of uncompetitive Italian companies, analysts point to Natuzzi as an example of the unknown small- and medium-sized businesses that are fuelling Italy's export-driven recovery."*

The Need for Consolidation in Italy

With such a strong background, we would think the story and the growth of Natuzzi was secured.

However, Italian government grants that were initially devoted to stimulating the economy in the south were progressively reduced (from 35% to 6%). The immediate consequence of this was an increase in labour cost (+24.74%), which encouraged the company to consider how to better benefit from its economies of scale.

With 77 plants spread around Apulia and Basilicata, Natuzzi faced a challenge with regard to economies of scale and logistic inefficiencies, due to the lack of infrastructure in the area. This encouraged the company to investigate where efficiencies and savings could be made. And on numerous occasions, Pasquale urged for the need to *"defend the company's future and think how to reduce costs in all areas"* in the in-house magazine.

---

56   November 1997, available at http://www.forbes.com/forbes/1997/0811/6003070a.html

57   Marcial, Gene G. "Natuzzi: An Undiscovered Italian Gem," *Businessweek*, 8 August 1994, p. 65. Retrieved from http://www.bloomberg.com/news/articles/1994-08-07/Natuzzi-an-undiscovered-italian-gem

58   Fuhrman, Peter, "Leather Man," *Forbes*, 7 November, 1994, pp. 296-297.

59   Crescere Insieme 23/97, page 19.

60   Kathleen M. Berry, "Skin Game - Thanks to Industrie Natuzzi, Leather is now within reach," *Investor's Business Daily*, 23 May 1994.

61   Lisa Bannon, "Natuzzi huge selection of leather funiture pays off," in *The Wall Street Journal*, 17 November, 1994.

This was the genesis of the 'Natuzzi 2000' project. Through this project, the company aimed to: *"Consolidate operations, rationalize presence, increase sales per customer and reduce the number of products: this will simplify the production, reduce the number of indirect resources and increase quality, productivity and efficiency. In other words, we will be lighter, more agile and so more competitive."*

The vision of the project was to build the 'City of Sofa', a 20,000-square-metre space to aggregate all production premises (one in Jesce, close to Santeramo, and two in Matera) to one location. Pasquale saw this as an opportunity to overcome some of the issues, such as *"structural shortcomings that continue to mean additional costs and therefore difficulty setting to remain competitive."*[62]

"Through this investment, we will gain great advantages: we will eliminate diseconomies for the transport of raw materials (semi-finished rubber materials, drums, leather, fabric) and we will reduce production costs and achieve an improvement in competitiveness and quality of our products."[63]

This ambitious project required a huge financial effort from the company: 1,100 billion ITL (equivalent to around 570 millions euros). It was financed through a 60% contribution from the company and 40% through public grants; this was the first time the Natuzzi Group had used public grants.

When Carlo Azelio Ciampi, Minister of Finance and Treasury, visited the plant, he said to a journalist that the company was, *"A confirmation that great ideas and initiatives in the south of Italy can be transformed into big successes!"*

Where 70% of other local manufacturers were small and inefficient, the Natuzzi 2000 project offered a successful strategy in addition to make-to-order production and a high level of productivity. The ability to fulfil the high demands generated was strengthened by a workforce that shared the founder's vision.

Pasquale shared his enthusiasm about the project with all the employees and was able to galvanize them during the annual convention. *"The new plants are at the forefront: each workstation, in the sewing departments, cutting and assembly, is equipped with a personal computer, allowing the operator to view the model they are working on and the relevant technical data sheets on their monitor ... In the first two months of 1997, already two plants have been set up ... What this company can do is miraculous!"*[64]

However, it was during these years that the competitive arena became quite problematic and challenging. Pasquale sensed these difficulties and prepared his plan. But, unfortunately, this was not enough.

In one of his Christmas speeches, he emphasized that, *"Our creativity is our main defence. But this is not enough. We are engaging in improving our organization, reducing costs and wastes that can affect the final price, because we want to offer affordable products to our customers. The market is challenging us, and we can win these battles only if we all are able to apply our best and work as a team. But, more than anything else, we need to defend our company from unfair competitors who can harm our future. Dear employees, our sense of responsibility in our daily work, our commitment to not divulging confidential company information to anyone who asks, are beyond words, and we can hope for a prosperous future."*

---

62   Pasquale Natuzzi in Crescere Insieme, vol. 16, Jan/Feb 1996, page 1.

63   Pasquale Natuzzi in Crescere Insieme, vol. 17, March/Apri 1996, page 1.

64   Crescere Insieme, vol. 20, Sept/Oct 1996.

Divani & Divani advertising, 1995

Natuzzi Institutional Campaign, 1997

Pasquale Natuzzi during the NYSE listing event in 1993

Pasquale Natuzzi receives the Leonardo Award from the Italian President
of the Republic Oscar Luigi Scalfaro, 1995

Automatic Guided Vehicles used at Natuzzi in 1990s

Pasquale Natuzzi at High Point building opening ceremony, 1998

Natuzzi's American Headquarters, High Point, North Carolina

CHAPTER 6

THE YEARS OF GLOBALIZATION TO REMAIN LOCAL

(2000-2003)

"Dream products can only be produced here, where the best craftsmen live, the best minds are, the most technical experts work. Abroad, we are going to face competition that has taken us out of the game, in a market created by us: the contemporary sofa in leather, offering the best quality/price ratio. That casual couch that has conquered the hearts of millions of consumers around the world. In short, we are going abroad to reclaim the market that has been taken away from us. Nothing more."[65]

Between 2000 and 2003 were the years when Natuzzi needed to reinvent itself. Once again, this was a revolution period for the company. On one side, the revenues were still high, but on the other, costs were increasing and eroding margins.

All efforts were put into the Natuzzi 2000 consolidation project, but it became evident that this alone was not sufficient for the company to move ahead, and a new solution was required.

Although the Natuzzi 2000 project tried to reduce costs through consolidation, some of the external factors that were positively influencing Natuzzi's performance in the 90s were coming to an end: the oil prices were increasing, the costs of raw material were growing and exchange rates became adverse for Italian exports.

The increase in the price of oil affected the marketing expenses and the transportation costs, since Natuzzi was located far away from its primary markets. The increase (+14%) in the cost of raw materials and, in particular, leather, polyurethane foam, polyester fibres and chemicals, had a negative effect on costs. The cost of raw leather rose mainly due to diseases in the cattle industry, such as foot-and-mouth disease and mad cow disease.[66]

Without going into the technicalities, the following chart shows the deterioration of the gross margin out of revenues. This indicator

---

65   Pasquale Natuzzi in Crescere Insieme, vol. 35/2001 page 13.
66   Annual report 2000, page 27.

expresses the percentage of sales after all costs of getting a product or a service to market are deducted. Essentially the higher the percentage, the better.[67]

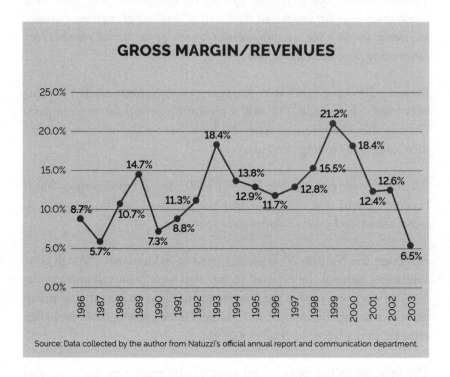

GROSS MARGIN/REVENUES

Source: Data collected by the author from Natuzzi's official annual report and communication department.

In 2000, the government and EU program that provided the group's tax exemption also expired. The tax rate increased from 19.8% to 24.3% in the same year.

Additionally, exchange rates become damaging to international trade, and in particular, as the euro became stronger than the US dollar. Exporting goods produced in Europe became much costlier compared to competitors located elsewhere.

The following figures show these changes in detail. The first figure shows the variation of exchange rates (ITL and euro versus US dollar) and net income ratio (net income/revenues).

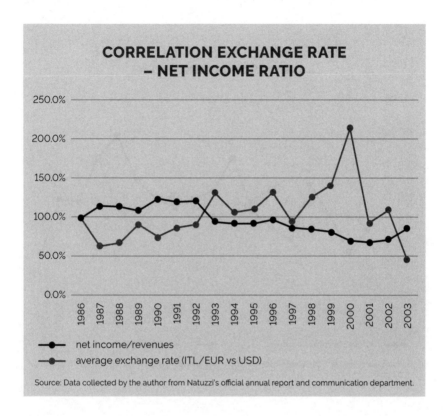

By looking at this figure we can see that when the currency Natuzzi was operating with (Italian Lira or euro) was weaker than the US dollar (black line around 100% or less than 100%), the revenues (grey line) were positively affected. When the Italian Lira or euro became more appreciated, the effect is the opposite and it pushes foreign operators to buy from companies using other currencies.

The second figure correlates the variation of oil price (grey line) with the variation of gross margin (black line). It shows that an increase in oil prices (grey line going up) erodes the margins as they become negatively affected. And a reduction in the price of oil produces a positive variation in the gross margin.

---

67 https://books.google.ch/books?id=6KPiEExbc7MC&pg=PA255&dq=gross+margin+ratio+meaning
    &hl=it&sa=X&ved=0ahUKEwjFtrCbgurPAhUnKsAKHaAzDE8Q6AEIQzAF#v=onepage&q=gross%20
    margin%20ratio%20meaning&f=false

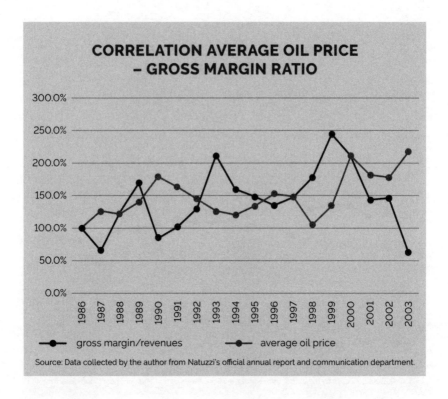

CORRELATION AVERAGE OIL PRICE – GROSS MARGIN RATIO

Source: Data collected by the author from Natuzzi's official annual report and communication department.

On top of these factors, global affairs further affected the company, especially after the September 11 crisis in 2001, when Natuzzi still had its strategic order backlog, but the overall economic outlook was bleak. This meant that Natuzzi had to reduce overtime hours for employees and terminate relationships with some subcontractors.

As discussed earlier, the strength and commitment of Natuzzi's employees was key to its success, and Pasquale emphasized this in an interview: *"There is a performance ratio of people, linked to speed in terms of quantity and quality, which is very high. Our employees are 30% more productive than the national average and the rate of absenteeism is equal to 2.9%. The people here live work as the conquest of a normality they never had in the macro economic context where they live, they feel fulfilled and all this translates for the company into a strong competitive advantage."*[68]

However, the high productivity of the group on its own was not sufficient to drive growth, given the unfavourable circumstances at that time.

Pasquale's Answers

Though Natuzzi's revenues were still high, Pasquale felt that the company deserved more and, taking these circumstances into consideration, he was encouraged to reinvent his company once again.

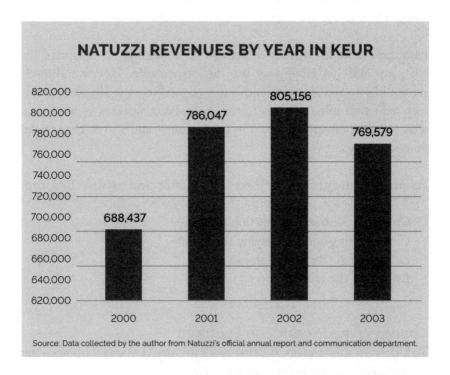

NATUZZI REVENUES BY YEAR IN KEUR

Source: Data collected by the author from Natuzzi's official annual report and communication department.

The founder used the in-house magazine to clearly express his vision going forward: *"Twenty years of specialization in the leather sofas segment and five years of experience in the fabric segment, a well-established global leadership, a unique ability to create new trends in the furniture industry. These are some of the strengths with which we get ready, in our 40th year of activity, to face the future with determination and enthusiasm, aware that competition in the world market is increasingly tough and selective."*[69]

---

68 Gilli D., "Interventi per lo sviluppo locale nel Mezzogiorno e ruolo della formazione. Rapporto 2000, ISFOL", Monografie sul mercato del lavoro e le politiche per l'impiego n.5, pp. 61-69.

69 Crescere Insieme, Vol 33/99, page 13.

The fierce competitive pricing in the market limited the company's capacity to adjust price lists to offset rising costs.[70] At that time, the company's revenue growth started to slow down, from 22% in 2000 to 14% in 2001, 2% in 2002 and then -4% in 2003. Pasquale had strong, clear views on this: *"There is a need to focus on creativity and corporate image. The price war is a loser."*[71]

Pasquale's sense of urgency to act and do something to safeguard his company and his employees was understandable. He gave himself six months to reduce costs and improve productivity. The key to this cost-reduction initiative was to reduce 'indirect workers' – employees who were not directly involved in production – and also to change the production mix.

Pasquale's strategy to combat these unfavourable circumstances included:

- Changing Natuzzi's production footprint
- Consolidating and simplifying the brand
- Launch of the decorator project
- Launch of the brand project

Changing the Production Footprint

To kick-start this strategy, the first inevitable decision was to shorten the production footprint in order to lower costs.

"After the attack on the Twin Towers, there was a surge of production in the Far East and China. In only a few years, this region had become the world's factory, with products more or less comparably with ours, but definitely priced lower," recalled Giuseppe Desantis, general manager of Natuzzi Group at that time.

"There were huge discussions about what to do. I remember that, in the end, we all agreed on the need to use our know-how. Performing our job in San-teramo or Shanghai or Brazil or Romania does not make any difference to us: we should reaffirm our leadership safeguarding the 'made in Italy' quality and, at the same time, reinvest the profit from low-cost productions in financing the new brand project.

This was not an easy task, and we had to convince the whole company that, in hindsight, this was the right thing to do."[72]

Natuzzi, in fact, decided to respond to the market by opting for an offensive strategy and, in 2001, chose to open new plants in Brazil, China and Romania. The first important task was to find a location for production.

A veteran employee Antonio Ventricelli, told me about this period with these words: *"I recall the president phoned me on a Saturday morning. We were discussing the progress of a project, but then he said to me, 'Antonio, I don't believe you are going to finish this project, because I have another important mission for you: we have to open a new production plant abroad and we have thought of you. Before giving an answer, please first find out if your family will support this move.'*

"I didn't need to think about it twice: I said, 'I'm in.'

"I had two kids at that time and I assured Mr Natuzzi that my family would support me on this project. I left Santeramo with Pinuccio Desantis, we met our commercial partners and visited locations in Shanghai. All the plants we visited were dilapidated, and the working conditions were very different from those I had left behind. Once we chose the plant in Shanghai, I had the task of producing a sofa called 'model 100', with the makeshift equipment available. The knowledge I had acquired in the field helped me succeed, and we then sent this sofa back to Mr Natuzzi, who checked this sofa and said, 'Well done. What do you need to start the production out there?'

"My response was simply, 'I only need a carpenter, a blacksmith and a couple machines for sewing and curling.' Within a month, we started."[73]

The production in China was in a location close to Shanghai and had the capacity to produce 700 seats a day.

---

70   Annual Report 2001, page 7.

71   Pasquale Natuzzi in Martellotta B., Gazzetta del Mezzogiorno, 10 November, 2002.

72   Giuseppe Desantis, interview performed in January 2017.

73   Antonio Ventricelli, interview performed in January 2017.

This was replicated in Brazil, where 14 employees were sent to Salvador de Bahia to set up the new production plant. And, as a father would give his children words for guidance, Pasquale gave each one these employees the following letter.

"Dear friend,

Before you leave, just as I would with a son or a daughter facing a trip and experience of a lifetime, I feel the need to share with you some concepts that I hope you keep in mind during your stay in Salvador de Bahia.

First of all, I would like to remind you that you're now involved in a very important mission. You are moving far and into a poor country with a great asset: your 'know-how'. You will realize the value of the work you have learned over the years as you train our new Brazilian employees.

You will see the reality of a lack of jobs, and you will understand the reasons that led me to inspire you to work hard, with love, and to make things in the right way. These are, in fact, the conditions to produce quality products, which sell successfully and allow a company to grow and generate wealth.

Our mission remains the same: to give work to young people, to generate wealth, to grow the territories in which we operate, without barriers and without borders. In a period where everybody is talking about globalization, we globalize our mission, aware that this allows us to grow here in our land, because we will improve our competitiveness and strengthen our market positions.

Last recommendation: please be always gentle, patient and tolerant with people who have a different mentality from yours, since you are a guest in that place.

Take care of yourselves and do a great job!

See you soon,

Pasquale Natuzzi"

At the same time production started in Brazil, two new production sites were set up in the south of Italy near Taranto, in Ginosa and Laterza. The purpose of these new sites was to boost production capacity by a further 1,800 seats a day.

The new plant in Brazil expanded rapidly and, in 2002 at its full capacity, the plant employed 350 people and turned out 750 seats a day.

To add to this collection of production plants, a new plant of 59,000 square metres was also built in Romania.

With this crucial change in its footprint, Natuzzi was transformed into a global player with a real global presence, several production sites in different countries and 36% of its workforce outside Italy. The increase in production capacity abroad proceeded hand-in-hand with manufacturing investments in Italy. After the 10th site in Italy was opened, Pasquale was recognized as, *"The man from the south who employs the north of Italy."*[74]

This succeeded in closing the gap between the production area and the final markets and to be positioned closer to both the final customers and to the raw material markets. From the new plant in Brazil, the company could serve the East Coast of the US, while the facility in China served the West Coast of the American continent. The plant in Romania allowed Natuzzi to easily reach the majority of the European market. The savings derived from these overseas operations enabled Natuzzi to produce furniture at much more competitive prices and to capture additional market share in the promotional segment of upholstered furniture.

While executing this strategy, there was also a need to keep the whole 'family' tied up together and make sure all employees understood the need for it.

---

74   Crescere Insieme, vol. 34/2000.

Despite all this growth, it was not an easy period for the company and not all the employees embraced the growth and expansion. The Italian colleagues felt that the those employees involved in the set-up of plants abroad were traitors, but the leaders at Natuzzi saw the value of this expansion. Given the market conditions, Antonio Ventricelli stated, *"Since we no longer had the competitive advantage in Italy, we had two options: one was to go abroad and start producing the cheaper private label, the other was to stop producing it. If you consider that profits coming from China are being reinvested back here in Italy, you will see that this is a good decision and the fact that Natuzzi is still alive today is thanks to this decision."*[75]

During one of the Christmas parties of this time, Pasquale chose the slogan, 'The future is here', with a clear emphasis on the importance of having a presence in Italy, and in Apulia in particular. So, although moving part of the production abroad fitted with the overall market situation, the company had no intention of moving out of Italy. *"Here we are building Natuzzi's future, which will become synonymous with good taste in interior design,"* said Pasquale, as he was sure about this future.

The glue to support the company in the globalization journey was once again the management of human resources. Michele Bonerba, the first HR and organization director at Natuzzi, retired and a new manager was hired externally (coming from Electrolux). The company showed that the people were still at the heart of Natuzzi when the employees participated in strike action for the first time. The company had tried to sell Natex, the company of the group involved in the polyurethane cutting process, but the employees were concerned about the solidity of the buyer. So, the shared governance of the company drove Natuzzi to put a stop to it and safeguard the future of its employees.

This strong commitment to employees, their development, low personnel turnover and absence of disputes showed that human resources management was a priority and that this was key to the company's success. These practices were noticed by the University of Bari, in Southern Italy, and Pasquale was awarded an honorary degree in Educational Science in 2001.

This was justified by the vision of human resources as a strategic lever to develop the company. During his keynote speech, Pasquale spoke of high hopes for the company's future: *"Our ambitious target is, in ten years from now, when anyone anywhere in the world wants to buy a sofa, they say, 'I want to buy a Natuzzi'. Yesterday we were good sofa producers, and today we need to continue producing high-quality sofas while transferring emotions through our history and our brand."*

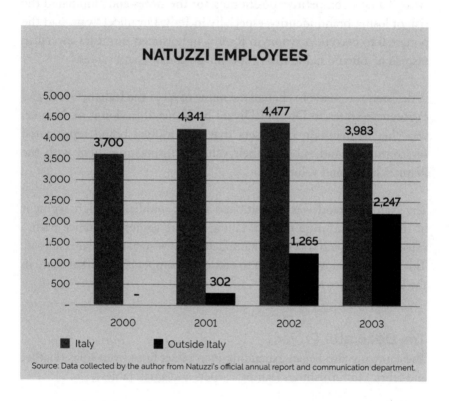

NATUZZI EMPLOYEES

Source: Data collected by the author from Natuzzi's official annual report and communication department.

---

75   Antonio Ventricelli, Natuzzi employee since 1975, interview performed in January 2017.

Consolidation of Brands

Another part of Pasquale's response to the harsh market conditions and competitors consisted of consolidating and simplifying the Natuzzi brands.

In particular, for Divani&Divani stores, the strategy was focused on building a strong and unequivocal bond with the Natuzzi brand. This created a new competitive positioning for the stores and eliminated the risk of losing brand identity, especially in Italy. Divani&Divani had the potential to become a synonym for any upholstered furniture specialist, instead of a brand name with a specific personality and values.

A decision was made to change the name of all of the Italian, Greek and Portuguese stores to Divani&Divani by Natuzzi. In doing so, Natuzzi was able to maintain the assets that the original brand represented for consumers and enhance their value by associating them with the Natuzzi brand and values.

The Natuzzi brand was repositioned in the middle- to high-segment of the global furniture market, taking a more aggressive stance with a private label, which was to be manufactured at several new plants abroad. This private label was designed to erode the competitors' market share in the low-end price segment.

The Decorator Project

The company also began expanding its product lines from sofas (leather and fabric) to furnishings (lamps, carpets and small tables).

At this stage, a greater focus was placed on furnishings, and it became the core of the new strategy. It offered customers a single shop where they could buy their desired sofa and also find furnishings that matched and coordinated. The goal was to offer complete lines of living room furniture that addressed consumers' varying tastes and lifestyles.

At Natuzzi stores and galleries, interior decorators created coordinated living room sets by matching various styles of sofas and armchairs with tables, lamps and rugs, all created by Natuzzi's world-class furniture designers, offering a harmonious living room in which each individual object perfectly matched with balance and Italian taste. For the Decorator Concept to take root in the minds of consumers – a complete living room solution with a high degree of aesthetic value – dedicated display areas that enhance the beauty and harmony of the proposed design solutions were employed.[76]

With this initiative, Pasquale again focused on beauty, harmony of space and elegance. He explained that in order to create a harmonious living space, *"You need expertise, knowledge, love of a parent, sensitivity of an artist and the rigor and thoroughness of a researcher."*[77]

This was a win-win situation and also benefited the Divani&Divani dealers. On one hand, they simplified the customers' experience and on the other, it provided the dealers with the opportunity to buy the whole concept from Natuzzi – sofa plus accessories – eliminating the need to go to different vendors for these furnishings.

During these years, Natuzzi drove a cultural change in people's behaviour, especially in Western countries. Living rooms moved from a formal environment for guests to an informal place to stay in, to enjoy friends and family, to surf the web, to relax or work in.

Sofas and armchairs started to evolve, allowing consumers to use them in a variety of ways. Natuzzi's sofa collection expanded to include additional functionalities such as beds, manual or electric recliners, and massage functions.

The Brand Project

The fourth pillar in the new strategy was the brand project. Pasquale wanted to change the perception of his brand. He saw Natuzzi as more than just a furniture manufacturer. *"Natuzzi adds style, personality and harmony to people's homes. Like a fashion designer who gives personality and*

---

76   Annual Report 2000, page 7.
77   Crescere Insieme, 2001, page 7.

harmony to those who wear his creations, Natuzzi adds style with fabrics, leather, the most innovative materials."

The brand project had two clear goals: to grow revenues and to re-establish Natuzzi as the leading provider of leather upholstered furniture.

The plan was to better penetrate the wealthier markets and create a barrier to entry for any eventual low-cost competitors coming from other countries. By creating a clear connection between the products and the brand, Natuzzi would underline its brand identity and establish a place in customers' minds.

However, changing a brand perception and repositioning it was not an easy undertaking. To do this successfully, the company sought to establish dedicated display spaces to house its product offerings. Accordingly, Natuzzi-branded stores and galleries – shops within the shops – became exclusive points of distribution. The living rooms on display were elegant and had a warm atmosphere, and each display expressed a different lifestyle, reflecting the personality and values of different customer tastes and needs.

Eventually, Natuzzi-branded furniture was only sold through Natuzzi-branded stores, which gradually replaced the Divani&Divani brand used in Greece, Spain and Venezuela.[78]

Natuzzi stores started to offer a full set of interior decoration services. Coordinated by Pasquale, this involved a team of product managers and decorators from the Design Centre. They designed harmonious furnishing solutions by combining sofas and armchairs with various styles and coverings, accessories and decorations, enhanced by certain features – a variety of cushion sizes and shapes, in different colours and materials that reflected the latest trends. These furnishing solutions were studied down to the smallest details. And thanks to a choice of around 40 different finishes, even the colours of the wooden feet could be carefully selected to coordinate with the coverings and accessories.

These activities gradually changed the visual identity of the company. The new logo and the colours of the leather made Natuzzi sofas famous worldwide. The logo was substantially redesigned to a clean and elegant look, with distinctive curved lines recalling the values of comfort and softness. The woodland and sage green colours chosen represent harmony, balance, well-being and relaxation. The 'U' in the middle of the logo was highlighted using a different colour and font, referred to 'you', expressing Natuzzi's consumer-centric mission. *"Natuzzi is you, your tastes, your desires, your expectations, your lifestyle,"*[79] said Pasquale.

EVOLUTION OF THE LOGO
AS PART OF THE BRAND PROJECT

Natuzzi	NATUZZI	NATUZZI
Logo until 2001	Logo from 2001 - 2011	Current logo, since 2011

Next, the company focused on communication, and a new strategy that worked on several layers was developed:

- Pure branding: the corporate level of communication that conveyed the brand philosophy. This focused on the relationships that grow between people and their living rooms;
- Product branding: this level aimed to raise the exclusivity of Natuzzi products. The focus of these communications was specifically products whose aesthetic and functionality were key selling points and could be promoted from time to time;
- Store attractions: this level of communication aimed to attract consumers to the point of sale with a variety of initiatives (announcements of new openings, promotions and events);

---

78   Annual Report 2000, page 7.
79   Annual Report, 2001, page 37.

- In-store communication: aimed to use language and content consistent with that used outside the point of sale, thus providing a shopping experience in line with the 'spirit of the brand'.

The new visual identity, communication and display system were presented during the Cologne International Furniture Fair in January 2002 and received extremely positive and encouraging reactions.

The drive for growth and expansion progressed with investment in R&D. While at the beginning of the 90s only a few dozen people were involved in R&D, with the opening of the first Natuzzi Design Centre in 2000, this number increased to 150. This was a dedicated think tank made up of creative personnel, such as designers, interior decorators and colour experts, as well as product specialists like regional product managers, market analysts and marketing managers. The centre produced 109 new models, 11 new leather products, 82 new colours and 33 new living room sets.

With the success of the first, a second Natuzzi Design Centre opened in Milan a couple years later. This was important for Pasquale, since he valued collaboration with external designers and wanted his employees to be influenced and educated by external views. And the centre in Milan enabled their creative development to be in direct contact with Italy's 'cradle of design'. They would benefit by interacting with the major Italian and international designers who choose Milan as a testing ground for new product concepts. And among its diverse activities, the Design Centre created an almost limitless combination of furniture models and furnishing accessories that made up different decorating concepts.

Key to the success of the brand project was that Natuzzi had full control downstream, through to the market. The company established an aggressive plan, which involved the opening of new Natuzzi galleries and stores. In total, 250 new galleries and 40 Natuzzi stores were planned for 2003 alone.

At the same time, the group reinforced its presence in the most strategic markets through opening new trading offices abroad: Natuzzi Nordic in Copenhagen, Natuzzi Benelux in Brussels, Natuzzi Iberica in Madrid and Natuzzi Switzerland in Zurich. These offices operated alongside the existing locations of Natuzzi Americas in High Point and Natuzzi Asia in Hong Kong. In line with this market expansion, the group purchased Kingdom of Leather, a chain of 15 shops in the UK, in 2003.

Pasquale's strong leadership was exactly what the company needed to be able to turn around disruptive periods, similar to those experienced by Natuzzi. *Forbes* gave the company a position on the 'magnificent 200' list: a short list of 20,000 small- and medium-sized enterprises that have distinguished themselves through their growth and company culture. Only three other Italian companies were on this list: Bulgari, Campari and Ducati. Article headlines stated, *"Not often does one person almost single-handedly revolutionize an industry. Here's one of them."*[80]

Recognised as Italy's second richest man in 2002 – the first being Giorgio Armani – Pasquale felt full responsibility for his company. On many occasions, he engaged national newspapers to help in asking the Italian government for a reduction in the cost of labour, through incentives that would provide local companies with breathing space and enable them to keep production local.

Despite the expansion and strategic development, and the fact that the number of seats manufactured each year continued to grow, economically the company's margins at the end of 2003 were decreasing by around 5.5%.

---

80 *Forbes* (2002), May 27, page 42.

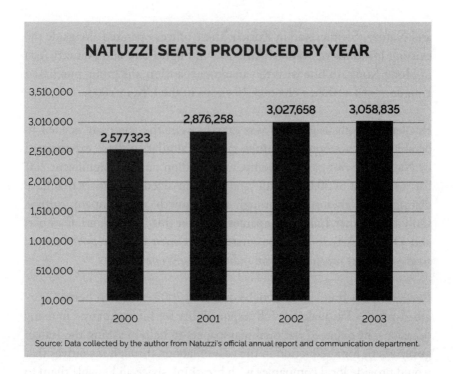

NATUZZI SEATS PRODUCED BY YEAR

Source: Data collected by the author from Natuzzi's official annual report and communication department.

At this stage, Natuzzi decided to make a big investment to reshape its future. In 2003, 72 million euros were spent on big initiatives that included:

- €15 million on improving the existing distribution network, opening 39 more Natuzzi stores and 256 galleries worldwide;
- €10 million on the branding project;
- €29 million on advertising campaigns;
- €18 million on improving production capacities.

Clearly, €72 million was a lot of money for a company the size of Natuzzi, and it was only made possible by the wise decision the company made in reinvesting the majority of its net income back into company expansions.

In the 2003 annual report, Pasquale declared that the group's competitive advantage depended on its innovation, internationalization, creation of Natuzzi brand value, lower costs and greater efficiency at all levels. He made it clear that the investments and the experience acquired within international markets in the previous 45 years would allow the company to continue with its mission of making design, quality and luxury easily accessible to all.

Despite the success that Natuzzi had achieved in its first 45 years, in 2003, 345 people were made redundant and temporarily laid off for two years. *"I do not want to put anybody at the door. I ask my colleagues to accompany me during this time uphill."*[81]

The situation was serious at Natuzzi, and there were repercussions in the whole district. Reporting on this situation in December 2003, a local newspaper ran the headline, *"The lights go out in Santeramo".*[82] The article focused on the lack of funds from Natuzzi to sustain the local initiatives through Christmas.

Though this was a tough decision for Natuzzi, the reality was that the company needed to reserve its energies and focus on the future. It needed to roll up its sleeves and show the market all the strength and creativity it was capable of.

The Answer of Other Companies in the District

At the beginning of the new millennium, the district reached a stage of maturity characterized by the presence of some great business leaders, who guided and oriented a network of small- and medium-sized enterprises linked to them by a basically stable and highly structured system of relations.

Three possible new roads emerged at that time:

- Focus on growth: companies focused on growth identified medium- to long-term development projects, investment programs in Italian and foreign distribution, internationalization of the production aimed at protecting the supply and demand markets;

---

81 Borrillo M., Corriere del Mezzogiorno, 12 December, 2003.
82 La Gazzetta del Mezzogiorno, 13 December, 2003.

- Focus on consolidation: companies tended to readjust their internal organization, strengthening the market relationship and trying to position their brand at the high end;
- Focus on renovation: companies tended to invest in diversification of production and internationalization of their footprint to take advantage of cheap labour costs and raw materials.

According to some surveys done at that time by the University of Basilicata, two important outcomes emerged. First was the fact that many companies, especially the small ones, were in standby, waiting for the big one to make some decisions and show the way forward.

Second was the willingness to make a change, which meant 21% of companies invested in the brand, in the image of the company and in enriching the product itself, in intangible values that can differentiate it from the one cheaper from the global competitors.

However, when we look at the way companies would have financed their programs, what is clear, in particular, was that companies referred mainly to resources obtainable through regional and European funding and, secondly, to their own equity.

Natuzzi decided to globalize its mission by opening production plants abroad to sustain the growth in Italy. He opted for the strategy of growth and renovation, but the rest of the district was slow to react.

"The district must be inspired by Natuzzi philosophy, not by its models," Pasquale stated in 2001. He identified the need for other companies in the district to create their own identities, their own characterization and also to diversify their products, avoiding the competition in the same niche market. This would help the whole district to move on and survive.

The big difference between Natuzzi's answer to the crisis and other leading companies was in the speed of reaction, in the relentless execution and the wider vision: Natuzzi first created its own distribution chain, through the Divani&Divani franchising program, then globalized its mission, opening production plants in locations with lower costs, and then focused on the brand project, pushing its brand in the upper end.

The idea of changing the logo, the dedicated private label, the payoff "It is how you live" were all ideas targeting the creation of an experience around the brand.

"Our strategy was ahead by five to six years compared to the others. Being listed, we gave visibility of our plans to the competitors, but they were simply following us, without a reasoned and rational choice, so they were opening shops in our locations just because we did so. All this has confused them and, at the end of the day, the competition was again only based on price. I was part of the district board, and we tried to work differently with the 'colleagues/ competitors', moving from an internal approach to a more cohesive approach, but there was a lack of foresight on the part of other companies and a general blindness by the district in understanding what was going on."[83]

Pasquale hunted around, found new avenues and pioneered them, trying new paths and showing other companies how to move. He behaved like an explorer. He said the entrepreneur is 'future-oriented' and guides his company to shelter from the storm in a new safe haven.

This was possible thanks to his deep understanding of the market and a strong willingness to succeed for his people.

---

83   Giuseppe Desantis, interview performed in January 2017.

Nexus model, designed by Studio Bellini, 2002

Brazil manufacturing plant, 2001

China manufacturing plant, 2001

Ginosa manufacturing plant, Italy,, 2001

Romania manufacturing plant, 2001

The leather warehouse at the Natuzzi plant in Laterza, Italy

Christmas Convention, 2001

Natuzzi Recieves an Honorary Degree from the University of Bari, 2001

CHAPTER 7

THE YEARS OF BRAND REVOLUTION

(2004–2010)

"The global market is like the ocean and we face it – just as in a long crossing – by sailing towards the future with unique strength and energy, sticking together during hard times and working closely towards common goals.

The high seas bewitch us with their infinite beauty and challenge us every day with their unexpected perils. We, however, know that our course is clear, just like our plans for the future. Whether it be under a calm, star-studded sky or battling the high waves of a storm, our team is ready to face whatever it must, in the knowledge that it will soon reach the safe haven of a port, ready to set sail at a moment's notice on new voyages of discovery."[84]

The years between 2004 and 2010 were characterized by a worsening of the financial crisis. But Natuzzi showed its tenacity and determination once again. Over this decade, the company's strategy was focused on two things: brand portfolio optimization and geographic/product diversification.

"We must realize that for a few years now, upholstered furniture companies have been focusing purely on production, the aim being to ensure optimization of costs and production lines. Now, this is no longer enough: the Murgia District must change its approach and diversify markets, as there will always be some foreign company able to sell a sofa at a lower price. To keep the heart of the company in Italy, it is necessary to raise the quality of the product; research, innovation and marketing are key areas to succeed."[85]

Natuzzi's mission was to make Italian style and quality affordable for all. Every year, 150 highly skilled professionals developed new projects based on market trends, from the initial idea to the creation of a new living room. The new collection was then launched, in a similar way a fashion designer releases their clothing designs.

Investment in R&D continued, as new materials and colours were continuously investigated to achieve the desired excellence. Pasquale coordinated all these efforts, and the result was a collection of 325 models, which would be updated each year with 100 new designs.

---

84 Pasquale Natuzzi in 2004 and 2005 Annual Reports.
85 Giuseppe De Santis, Gazzetta del Mezzogiorno, 24 October, 2004.

This led to the division of the Natuzzi brand into two separate lines:

- The top-of-the-range 'Pasquale Natuzzi Collection', now called Natuzzi Italia, which included the highest-quality products in terms of creativity, detail of design and choice of materials and finishes;
- The Natuzzi range, now called Natuzzi Editions, which, while at the middle of the price bracket, successfully embodied the various values of the brand, such as innovation, elegance, reliability and quality.

Both collections were divided into three styles – casual, urban and vintage – each aimed at customers with different lifestyles and aesthetic tastes. Casual was aimed at the younger customer, someone who loves freedom, whose home is informal in style and for whom comfort and functionality are essential. Urban was more of cosmopolitan and eclectic style, for those who love to surround themselves with extremely refined things. And vintage tailored to those who desire more traditional objects with a symbolic value.

The company managed a private label division, Softaly, dedicated to mass market dealers and the promotional segment of the market. Its products were manufactured in the group's factories located in China, Brazil and Romania. The aim of this product line was to sustain the growth of the rest of the company through its high volumes and low prices. Furthermore, the Style Centre designed a generous selection of complementary furniture (tables, lamps and rugs) and accessories (vases, containers/holders and candles), which allowed for a completely coordinated living room.

When explaining the unique and distinctive advantages of choosing a Natuzzi product to consumers, the stores became as crucial as the products. They were a place where Natuzzi could strengthen its presence in the market, increase its brand recognition and where consumers could get a 360° experience that included consulting on furnishings, purchasing and delivery.

Stores were located specifically in the trendiest areas in big cities around the world. These key locations were instrumental in being able to easily transfer these high-quality products with an Italian touch to local passers-by. And based on the maturity of the market, the company would decide whether the shop in that location should be a Natuzzi-owned shop or a franchisee. In both cases, agents were trained in a similar way.

Meticulous groundwork was put in by the company to fully understand the culture of countries, the dynamics of consumption and local competitors. This was then used to define the input and action plan required in each individual country. Essentially, the same attention to detail that was devoted to product development in the previous decade was now devoted to understanding markets and the required implementation strategy for success. Each store showcased the latest trends in interior design for those who wanted to enjoy quality and Italian style. The graph below displays the rapid growth of the company, starting from 19 stores in 2004 and increasing to over 300 in 2007. Likewise, the number of galleries grew from 126 to over 400 in 2007.

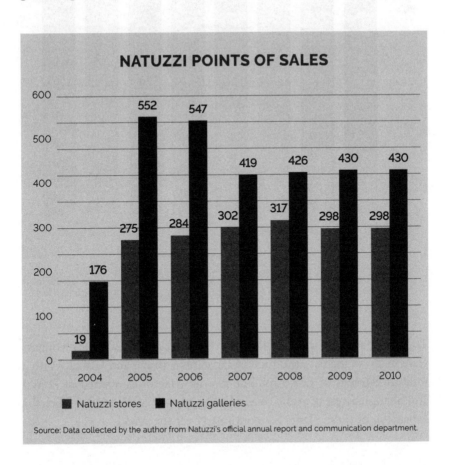

Source: Data collected by the author from Natuzzi's official annual report and communication department.

Throughout these years, the company saw fluctuations in the source of its revenues, as contributions from the private label increased from 20.9% to 43.5% in 2010. The chart below compares the annual percentage sales made through the private label and Natuzzi.

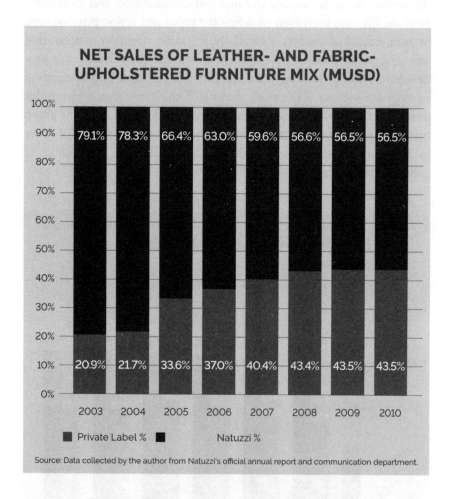

NET SALES OF LEATHER- AND FABRIC-UPHOLSTERED FURNITURE MIX (MUSD)

Source: Data collected by the author from Natuzzi's official annual report and communication department.

To further support the growth of the private label, in 2004 investments were made to increase production capacity in Brazil and China. With a total investment of €27.6 million, two new factories opened in Pojuca and Shanghai, respectively. To sustain the growth of the private label, the expansion of these plants has continued over the years.

Revenues of the different geographic market also saw a shift. Whereas the Americas were always the core market for Natuzzi, and its first love, they were becoming less relevant.

Looking at net sales presented in the graph below, the Americas lost 6% in favour of Asia, while Europe and the Middle East (EMEA) remained fairly stable, at approximately 52%.

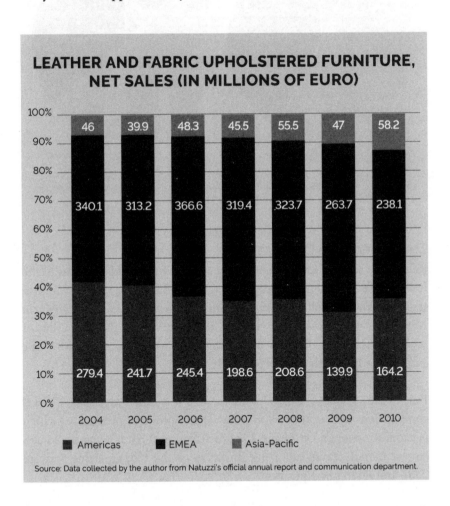

LEATHER AND FABRIC UPHOLSTERED FURNITURE, NET SALES (IN MILLIONS OF EURO)

	2004	2005	2006	2007	2008	2009	2010
Asia-Pacific	46	39.9	48.3	45.5	55.5	47	58.2
EMEA	340.1	313.2	366.6	319.4	323.7	263.7	238.1
Americas	279.4	241.7	245.4	198.6	208.6	139.9	164.2

■ Americas   ■ EMEA   ■ Asia-Pacific

Source: Data collected by the author from Natuzzi's official annual report and communication department.

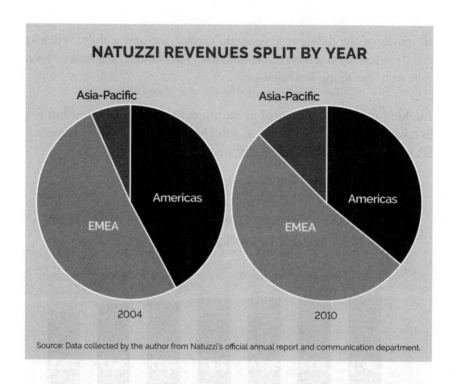

NATUZZI REVENUES SPLIT BY YEAR

Asia-Pacific   Asia-Pacific

Americas   Americas

EMEA   EMEA

2004   2010

Source: Data collected by the author from Natuzzi's official annual report and communication department.

The Rise of the Chinese Giant

Relocation seemed to be the only way to reduce the industrial cost of the Italian sofa. In 2004, Fabrizio Onida, a well-known Italian economist, stated, *"Only the most courageous companies, those that relocate seriously, will play a lead role in the global market."* He agreed with the relocation of production, where countries with lower costs would become part of the corporate strategy to compete globally.

But, in this scenario, a new phenomenon was emerging: that of price competition and counterfeiting by local Chinese producers, which became stronger and stronger. They swiftly moved from being the fourth largest manufacturer exporting furniture to the US, replacing Italy in 2004 and taking first position.

The chart opposite shows the official statistics gathered by the US Census Bureau for imports of upholstered household furniture from 2000–2010. It is shocking to see the rise of China's power and the decline of Italy's in this sector.

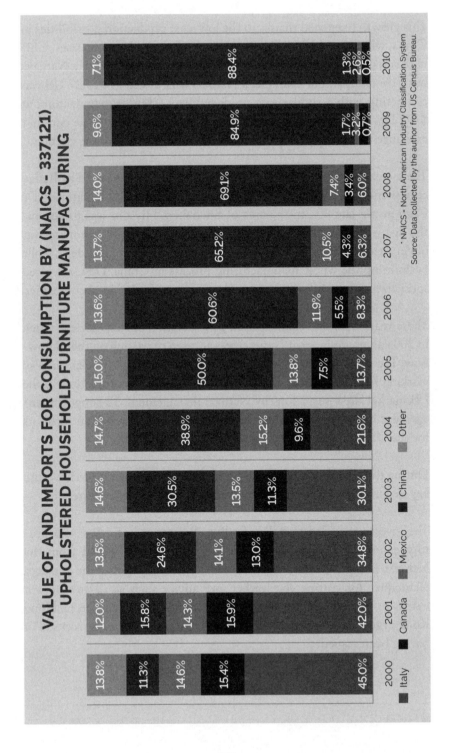

VALUE OF AND IMPORTS FOR CONSUMPTION BY (NAICS - 337121) UPHOLSTERED HOUSEHOLD FURNITURE MANUFACTURING

* NAICS = North American Industry Classification System
Source: Data collected by the author from US Census Bureau.

Italy · Canada · Mexico · China · Other

133

This growth happened thanks to the low-cost production possibilities in China, which resulted in high-volume production. In some cases, Chinese companies were able to produce and sell a sofa similar to a Natuzzi, but 51% cheaper. For example, a Natuzzi sofa priced at $1,627 US was competing with a similar sofa produced by a Chinese manufacturer at $799 US. According to Pasquale, this was partially due to the currency exchange rate and partially due to the economic system of the country.[86]

The increase of Chinese exports in this sector was also assisted by Italian entrepreneurs. One example is Luca Ricci. Luca opened his company De Coro in the late 90s, in the area of Shenzhen. His aim was to become the first worldwide leather sofa producer. The secret of his company was buying leather from countries with high costs (Italy and Sweden), while performing the whole manufacturing process in China. De Coro hired specialized personnel who were paid twice that of other local companies.

These years were also characterized by a violation of trade secrets, when in 2005 an ex-designer at Natuzzi was accused of passing on their know-how. The designer left Natuzzi in 2001 and became a freelancer, also working for a competitor. The unexpected rise of this competitor in the US market drew suspicions by Natuzzi management. To support management in investigating this, the company hired commercial directors for the US, Europe and Denmark.

During these years, Natuzzi even hired a private investigator to look into key ex-employees who were suspected of selling company secrets.

The investigation led to police finding illustrations of a few sofa prototypes on the freelancer's computer that had been copied from the Natuzzi Design Centre, together with emails explaining the projects, techniques for cutting the leather and advice such as, *"Don't make it exactly as the original."* In March 2005, the Court of Justice in Hong Kong urged the competitor to withdraw from sale the sofas accused of having been copied.

---

86   Lonardi G., Made In Italy alle corde, cosi i cinesi ci stritolano, La repubblica, 18 November, 2004.

But this example of violation of trade secrets was just one of many. There were many inspections when local Italian police found Natuzzi catalogues used for 'inspiration' in other external laboratories. In these inspections, the police also found employees of other companies working 14 hours a day without making any social contributions or taxes. This phenomenon was not only damning to the revenues of Natuzzi, but was becoming a critical factor for the government, as a black labour market that eluded taxes was emerging.

Discussing this problem in an interview, Pasquale explained that, *"Natuzzi would have strongly protected the know-how it had built in 46 years of activity, with the aim of continuing to promote Italian products and protecting jobs in Southern Italy."*

It was not only Natuzzi that was suffering from such counterfeiting activities; many other companies suffered in the same way. The requests to protect the 'Made in Italy' claim were coming not only from Natuzzi, but also from other big groups (i.e., Armani, Gucci and Luxottica), although politicians were slow to react.

Additionally, as companies from Southern Italy were moving to China, there was also a movement in the other direction. Chinese entrepreneurs were moving to Southern Italy in order to learn and attack the production directly at his heart.

In 2004, the local police in Matera reported that more than 3,000 Chinese immigrants were working in leather tanning and processing. The majority of these individuals had come from the north of China. They worked 24 hours a day on their own or for subcontractors of local products in the district.

It was true that Chinese companies were not directly competing with local Italian companies, but it was also true that their black economy and low production prices, together with a low level of attention to local legislation, generated a distortion in the market.

Italian companies in crisis believed that outsourcing part of their production to Chinese producers would help them overcome the 2004 financial crisis and stay in the market. But often this was only a temporary fix, since in the long run, the same Chinese companies were acquiring the know-how and the economic power to build their own production sites.

Pasquale's Battle to Resist

Pasquale became a warrior in the fight against counterfeiting. The *Financial Times*[87] referred to the situation of the furniture producers in Italy with a metaphor from the famous novel *I promessi sposi* (*The Betrothed*) by Alessandro Manzoni, a novel about foreign invasion, plague, famine and tyranny. *"Today, Italian producers are playing out a modern version of the struggle Manzoni described: defending Italy's historic leadership in the furniture business from outside threats."*

Pasquale Natuzzi tried to attract the attention of politicians and the media by running a dedicated campaign for the promotion of 'Made in Italy' and against the black market. This was for the benefit of the whole region, as well as his people.

He was not alone in Europe in this war. German and Spanish producers joined him in requesting that the European Union take anti-dumping measures against China and Vietnam. Though they knew that these measures would not save the companies that were in crisis, they would at least guarantee fair competition in the old continent.

The answer to China's domination was clear to many big players, such as Natuzzi: *"For a China that floods us, there is also a China to flood. We must beat them where they can never imitate us: in taste, in style, in details. In the culture of hard work and the flash of invention that results in a perfection and a uniqueness that makes 'Made in Italy' a worldwide valued success."*[88]

Pasquale was strongly convinced of his strategy. A brand can create loyalty, security and stability and can allow higher margins, despite the fact that many Italian brands are still strongly related to the genius of their founders.[89] In 2004, a Natuzzi customer reported in an article that he had approached the founder and told him, *"Pasquale, stop it. You Italians and the idea of producing sofas that are labelled 'Made in Italy'. You should give up. Now the Chinese are here. You, too, should produce your products in Asia. Or else you will not last long."* To which Pasquale did not hesitate to respond, *"You should understand that Natuzzi not only sells you a sofa, but it sells you a brand."*[90]

The year 2005 was a turnaround one for Natuzzi. Commenting on the 2005 financial results, Pasquale declared, *"I've made many mistakes. However, the lesson is now clear, and we will not repeat them again. After over 40 years of growth, our company has had a setback that has led to our first budget in the red. We lost in the Americas, but now we can move ahead, thanks to our productions in China and Brazil. We have made some errors in acquisition (i.e., Kingdom of Leather in the UK) where we did financial due diligence but not value due diligence. We are now ready to start again."*

This statement was the basis for new plans, which aimed to further improve efficiency and reduce operating costs by streamlining the corporate structure. A new, slimmer corporate structure was launched by merging eight companies, liquidating five companies and establishing a group holding company.

However, due to the reduction of orders, these activities were not enough. So, for the first time in its history, in May 2005, Natuzzi's management agreed on a restructuring plan for 415 employees. It was the first time the company had to face a dramatic change like this, but Pasquale decided to try all he could to limit the impact on his employees, while keeping in line with his own personal social mission as an entrepreneur.

This included further investments that would support the Natuzzi brand and considerably reduce its costs in all departments, with a particular focus on reducing costs in the Italian facilities.

---

87 *Financial Times*, 9 April, 2005, Designs of the future.

88 Lino Patruno, Gazzetta Del Mezzogiorno - Il domani nella fatica antica - Lino Patruno, 23 May, 2005.

89 Ernesto Illy, Il Mondo, 30 April, 2004, page 70.

90 Giuseppe De Tomaso, La Gazzetta del Mezzogiorno, 28 April, 2004.

At that time, Pasquale was in the US continuing to research orders made through Natuzzi's ten largest customers. Meanwhile, his management flew to Rome and met with the Italian Minister of Labour. Being a strong and passionate leader, Pasquale decided to trust his words to the columns of a newspaper article:[91]

"I want to strongly remind institutions that we should all be conscious, once and for all, of the risks of survival that our region and the Italian manufacturers face. The exposure to global competition of exports and penalization due to rigidity, charges and restrictions make it expensive for us to compete with emerging countries.

"Europe and Italy must decide quickly whether to give in or deny a future for manufacturing companies.

"Five years have passed since we at Natuzzi publicly stated, with courage and clarity, that the world was changing and that the shock wave of the competition from countries with low labour costs would have been much stronger.

"We said publicly that a change was necessary in the economic and fiscal policies of our country: more infrastructure, lower tax, reduction of labour costs, support to firms capable of performing projects to reposition itself and focus on quality. I remember the surprise even of my colleagues when they read my statement where I said that, without this care, the sofa district would die in just ten years.

"With regret I have to say that five years have not been enough for institutions to take action on the structural problems that hamper the competitiveness of Europe and Italy as emerging economies.

Our company continues to believe in the possibility of remaining and producing in the territory. But you cannot avoid being realistic and define this difficult and uncertain challenge because it is not only linked to the effectiveness of a business strategy, but rather bound to a complex connection of factors, not least the institution's ability to react in helping to sustain the investments of Natuzzi, designed to preserve as much as possible employment levels in Italy.

"In this we believe and to this we will continue to commit ourselves."

The restructuring plan included a temporary reduction of the workforce of 1,320 positions by the end of 2005, affecting all departments across the group. The plan aimed to reduce manufacturing costs in Italy and increase overall efficiencies so that the group could become more competitive, recover profitability through the closing of nonperforming retail units and regain market share, especially in the medium- to high-end part of the market. Here the group continued to invest in the Natuzzi brand.

This decision produced a protest without precedent in Natuzzi. The dialogue between management and employees had always been open and direct and the company had never faced union action before.

From six o'clock on the morning of 17 May 2005, 1,000 employees went on strike and protested in front of the plant in Santeramo, against the company decision. The tension level was very high and the first companies that were affected were the subcontractors, since they were dependent on orders from Natuzzi. Over the next few days, people continued to strike against the delocalization strategy. As a result, from 3–12 June the company had to stop production.

Although this was a difficult time, the situation was jointly managed by unions and the management, who decided to fight together rather than against each other. In a combined effort, they requested the Italian government take action, since this problem had been stressed for years before, but completely ignored.

The game that Natuzzi was playing was not an easy one.

Several economists supported his idea, and well-known journalist Federico Rampini wrote, *"Natuzzi is an outstanding enterprise. The only way of escaping the pursuit of emerging countries is to gain a reputation for quality, elegance and style, and by convincing the international customers to pay a premium for its products. Natuzzi has chosen to treat China not only as a source of manpower, but also as a vast market for sales through its shops."*[92]

---

91   La Gazzetta del Mezzogiorno, Pasquale Natuzzi, 18 May, 2005.

92   Federico Rampini, BARI - La crisi Natuzzi come si guarisce dal "male cinese" –Repubblica Bari, 28 May, 2005.

Federico believed that Natuzzi was doing the right thing and taking the right action *"moving quickly on the most prestigious and exclusive vocations, where the talents of 'Made in Italy' remain unmatched and revered by the whole world, including China. But this is a march that cannot be left to the forces of a single company, or of a single local community. We need a national direction, ideas and capital to accelerate the pace and help those in danger of being overwhelmed and crushed."*

Thanks to the accumulation of orders during the summer, the group decided to call back around 90% of the workers who had been temporarily laid-off from the Italian factories.

Pasquale was convinced that the Apulia district could overcome these problems, but that it needed more creative emulation and less destructive competition. He felt that small companies should join and get the critical mass necessary to compete together, and that the government should improve the logistics to reduce the time to market and support the company's investments in R&D and education.

In June 2006, in order to recover profitability and efficiency, specifically in its Italian plants, the group obtained an extension of the temporary workforce reduction for the next two years. The group agreed with the Italian unions that no more than 508 workers would be affected. At the same time, Natuzzi invested €10 million to consolidate its production into four plants, a reduction from the previous eight plants, which generated economic and organizational savings. The industrial plan of 2006–2008 culminated in the creation of one main production centre and one main logistic centre.

On 12 June 2007, the group announced that, in light of the continuous challenging business conditions affecting all major markets, and the adverse currency trends that were depressing the number of orders, it needed to temporarily reduce the production working time in its Italian plants, from eight to five hours per shift, for 13 weeks. The production site in Jesce was closed for the whole month of August, affecting 230 workers. This announcement was followed by a strong strike action in which 1,000 employees took part for three hours.

Once again, Pasquale decided to take action and wrote a letter to all of the employees, calling for a meeting on June 30 at the International Fair Pavilion in Bari. The idea behind this meeting was to go back to Natuzzi's roots and establish a moment where all employees had the opportunity to ask the founder, CEO and president of the company questions without any filters. The unions did not like this approach, since they had been fully bypassed. But this behaviour was seen to be acceptable, given the urgency of the situation, the importance of transferring a clear message to the employees and to encourage everyone to work together towards a common goal: relaunch Natuzzi and win the market competition.

The convention was attended by more than 2,000 employees, who had all been given the opportunity to pose a question to Pasquale via a form a few weeks prior to the event.

Afterwards, watching videos of the event, one can immediately see the feeling of urgency and the predicament that the company was in. Pasquale went on stage and started with these words, *"I am the founder of this company, I am the chairman, and together with my family we are the majority shareholder. I am the man who makes the decisions. If today we have problems, I am responsible, no one else."*

The opening of his speech had a strong message of humility and emphasized the message to his employees that they were all in the same boat. *"Since I founded Natuzzi in 1959, I have never given up the direct relationship with my employees. Social responsibility, dialogue and transparency are part of the DNA of our company."*

In this speech, Pasquale retraced the salient periods of the company's history, focusing on the difficulties and the way they had been overcome. He recalled the initial scepticism of those who did not believe it was possible to produce high-quality sofas in the south of Italy, an area that was economically undeveloped, but where optimism, willingness and determination were perhaps the strongest tools.

He also emphasized the importance of the brand revolution that was underway, which aimed to make Natuzzi the Louis Vuitton of sofas.

He denounced the fact that the institutions didn't assist this revolution, a revolution that required harmonious commitment from all, including the State, to succeed.

Responding to those who accused Natuzzi of using the State aids and then moving the company abroad, Pasquale shared some figures about the period between 1987–2006:

- The company invested €307 million in a production site and generated many jobs in the local communities;
- The total State grants and aids collected equalled €51 million, while through tax and social contributions the company paid back something like €697 million, 13.6 times more than what it had originally received from the State.

Pasquale confirmed that the company was more than solid and had €110 million ready to invest in the brand project.

He was convinced that the company could do it, and that the convention would help galvanize all participants. *"We are determined to pursue our strategies with the support of a management team that has international experience. The Natuzzi leather will change for the third time in 40 years."*

To show his commitment to the employees, Pasquale decided to sell his private jet, and he justified this decision by making the comment, *"Better to cut something than make debts."*

In May 2008, the group communicated a further extension of their temporary work force reduction in Italy, involving 1,200 positions for 12 months.

For the same reasons, the group announced layoffs at its Brazilian plants, involving about 570 workers, that the group hoped to recall in the next few months, if orders for the Brazilian plants began to recover.

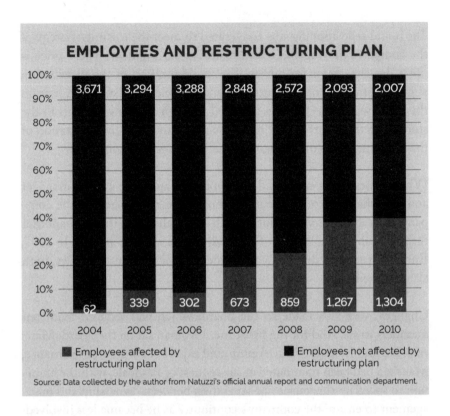

EMPLOYEES AND RESTRUCTURING PLAN

Source: Data collected by the author from Natuzzi's official annual report and communication department.

The Attempt of External CEOs

During these years, there was another revolution in Natuzzi's management – or at least an attempt at one.

Until 2006, Pasquale was fully involved in all strategic and operational decisions. In June of that year, he decided to step back and give the helm to an experienced, external manager to drive his ship out of the storm. The CFO of Bulgari, Ernesto Greco, joined Natuzzi and became its CEO. Famous for his ability to take a family company to the next level, Ernesto focused on the management of the company, while Pasquale became more involved as a stylist. This was quite historic for Natuzzi, since it was the first time that its founder had delegated his main responsibilities and power to an external manager.

The new CEO's plan was quite ambitious and stood on three pillars: brand repositioning, reorganizing distribution and revisiting productions.

The brand repositioning was accelerated to meet the existing strategy of the company, moving the brand to the upper segment, where price is not a decisive factor for buyers. The reorganization of the distribution aimed to strengthen the Natuzzi brand and clearly distinguish it from the lower segments. This was achieved through large investments in the stores. The third part, revisiting productions, involved reorganization of the different plants in order to rationalize the production chain.

When Ernesto was appointed, Giuseppe Desantis, the general manager and vice chairman of the board of directors for 22 years, left the company, since his role was reduced with these changes. This was another turning point in the history of Natuzzi, and he was just the first. In 2007, Enrico Carta, HR director, and Daniele Tranchini, head of sales, both also resigned.

Changes were also made to the board, which was reduced from ten members to six. And for the first time, a woman sat on the board: Maurizia Iachino Leto di Priolo. A profound expert of corporate governance, Maurizia had been nominated at the request of Pasquale, with the ambition to speed up the journey of separation between ownership and management to ensure the company's continuity as he became less involved.

Although the financials were still not very positive, investments in marketing and advertising continued. Having spent €7.1 million in 2006, Natuzzi was the top spender on advertising in Italy. Conversely, its spending on R&D left Natuzzi in the 29th position in Italy in 2007 for its R&D.

But, after one only year at Natuzzi, Ernesto resigned. This was a sign of a company where the founder had still a 'strong presence', because Ernesto found being in command to be a big challenge. Then, someone suggested that Pasquale follow Bill Gates' example: take a step back and leave the company in the hands of these expert managers. Clearly, this would not be easy for any self-made businessman.

In an interview in 2007, Pasquale explained that, *"Managers who decided to leave the company have not understood the connection between the company and the territories that it operates in. To reposition a brand, we need a deep cultural change. And some of our employees are not ready to do that yet, while other are already engaged. I told our top managers that we have a commercial mission, but also a social one, both of which are of equal importance. I feel I took commitments towards the local communities. I do not need managers to tell me that I should close everything and move all the productions to China. I know that myself. But I do not want to, and I will not do it. Challenge stays in finding new ways to remain in these territories.*[93]*"*

A clear sense of urgency emerged from 2005–2007 due to an accumulated loss of around €63 million. Unions pushed for full disclosure of the industrial plan and started to protest. Then, in 2008, with international experience at Nestlé and several other multinational companies, Aldo Uva was appointed as the company's new CEO.

Originally from Matera, Aldo first met Pasquale in 2000 and was convinced to join the company for two reasons: the first being that this was a company from his homeland and the second was the challenge of relaunching the Natuzzi Group. The determination of this new CEO appealed to the founder, since Pasquale believed in him and shared his values.

Aldo launched the new industrial plan called '11-1-15': the target was to achieve revenues of €1 billion by 2011 with a gross margin of 15% on sales, leveraging on self-financing to sustain growth. It was hoped that this focus would bring order back in to the company in 2009, establishing a new culture, and that 2010 would then be a year of acceleration and in 2011 the company would be focused on achieving its target.

Aldo's secret was using the right mix of employees, regionalizing the production, reducing costs and reducing debt generation to avoid financial loss.

He brought an American style of management to the company and set up the 'think bold team' with the aim to innovate and transform the company working on wide strategic projects, such as the Shanghai Expo, the 2015 Milan Expo fair and the London Olympics.

93　Pasquale Natuzzi in "Io non tolgo le tende", Nuova del Sud, 12 November, 2007.

In his tenure as CEO, he increased the managers in the six regions from four to 17. He moved away from the traditional organizational set-up, and the company saw some big changes. For example, the headquarters in Santeramo were no longer at the heart of the company and to increase the speed and agility, he employed more managers from multinationals who were all too aware of the fact that the best way to predict the future was to build it.

But, unfortunately, this winning streak came to an end in March 2009, after only eight months, when Aldo had to leave the company for personal reasons.

After Aldo's departure, Pasquale decided to stop employing external CEOs and returned to his position as CEO of Natuzzi. *"I only know how to do one thing and that is the thing I will keep on doing: producing sofas. And I will keep on doing it in Santeramo, Apulia. The storm will go away and I will be able to drive our boat to a safe harbour, since I know this boat and I know how to steer it."*

Pasquale Back in the Driving Seat

Natuzzi was an Italian asset and it needed to be defended, but the external circumstances were not easy to overcome. Pasquale continued his fight and, during the relaunch, the company did not forget about its employees, instead restructuring and offering training for 300 people. In 2009, a budget to spend €25 million on marketing and communication was approved. One third of this budget was dedicated to cultural events at Natuzzi stores, with the goal of transforming them from a point of sale to a place where the company brand could be developed. The remaining two thirds were dedicated purely to marketing and advertising.

But in 2010, he was forced to close a manufacturing plant in Jesce and a carpentry plant. At that time, 60% of the labour force was affected by restructuring. As a result, in June 2010, new sacrifices were announced:

- 1,400 employees directly involved in production were reduced to 540 indirect employees;
- Top managers cut their salaries by 20%;

- The CEO reduced his salary by 30%;
- Management buyouts and other incentives were cancelled.

These were temporary sacrifices, but were necessary in relaunching the business and enabling it to compete again. Reading the many documents published about Natuzzi during these years, it is clear that the company strongly believed it could overcome the many challenges it was facing. And Pasquale was reported to have said that he was tired of losing money and wanted to do his best to save the company.

In 2010, a new five-year business plan was initiated. This focused on brand consolidation, organizational restructuring, production units specialization, cost reduction and sacrifices for all.

A new product line was also launched, Natuzzi Editions, with the goal of generating the volumes necessary to sustain the group's production sites around the world. Natuzzi Editions was developed solely for wholesale distribution and contained a wide range of models and functionality, positioned for the medium- to low-segment of the market.

In a nutshell, Natuzzi's presence in 2010 in the different markets was as follows:

- Natuzzi Italia – high-end, high-quality products, 'Made in Italy' logos with detailed designs and customized materials and finishes targeted the very high end of the market;
- Natuzzi Editions – targeted the medium-to-low segment of the market;
- Private Label (Softaly) – targeted the low segment of the market.

The key for Pasquale when launching this new business plan was to get the buy-in from all key stakeholders so that it would get the official green light. The plan was shared with unions and institutions, because he felt it was crucial for both the management and all other employees to believe in it.

The Fall of the Murgia District
During these difficult times, the district was close to imploding.

Pasquale described it as a 'fratricidal war', companies killing each other with immorality and illegality. A strong message was also given to those employees who decided to leave the company to make more money by bringing their background to small local companies: *"By copying our models, they hurt us as a company, the industrial district and in the end themselves. In a global market, only those able to offer new creative solutions of good quality will survive. Thinking of competing with countries with lower costs makes no sense to me."*[94]

In July 2000,[95] Pasquale described this situation extensively with the following words:

"To create a sofa means to create a 'new' model, something that was not there before. But to create a sofa you have to know consumers' tastes, find a 'style' and give the product an identity, a personality. Not only that, but the methods of production for that model must be competitive. Finally, to ensure a long life, you need to promote it through advertising. All this requires creativity.

"But everything has a cost. And that's where I see the weakness of this industrial district. So far, most of this cost has been born by Natuzzi. Why is it just the Natuzzi Group that continues to 'create', guaranteeing continuity and building a future? Nearly all other producers in the district do not create; instead, they copy, even copy us, and sell less."

With this statement, Pasquale was highlighting the unfair competition of some of the local companies that were copying Natuzzi's designs and selling them at a cheaper price, sometimes up to 20% cheaper. Natuzzi had creative expenses, including R&D and advertising, but for these companies, the cost was only the production of the sofa itself.

This sort of unfair competition became even more aggressive outside Italy (i.e., China, Thailand, Korea, Brazil and East Europe), where products could be produced at an even lower cost. This generated a tough fight on prices.

---

94   Pasquale Natuzzi in *Crescere Insieme* 2000, vol. 34.
95   Crescere Insieme, vol. 34/2000, page 25.

Natuzzi's two main competitors, Calia and Nicoletti, created their own distribution channels, but at slower speeds than Natuzzi, while other companies like Contempo were mainly focused on the product itself and others, such as Chateau D'ax, used a different business model, in which production was entirely outsourced to subcontractors.

In 2005, Nicoletti moved its production to China and Moldova. However, it was too late. Redundancy and restructuring programs had spread across the companies and, in that year, Pasquale Natuzzi made a bold decision: to abandon the committee of the district, since he saw no further value in it.

The majority of the other companies (Nicoletti, Calia, Contempo) had a high debt ratio and consequently their ratings were decreasing, while Natuzzi was the only one without debts and therefore able to move forward.

In 2007, Calia and Softline, two historical competitors, created a partnership to compete together in the US market. This was a key moment, since the two companies realized they couldn't compete alone and, rather than killing each other, they created synergy. Calia's strength was the possibility to produce in China, while Softline had a commercial presence in the US, as well as the style and design knowledge.

A 2007 survey found that only 46 companies were left out of the 500 during the years of growth and 5,000 jobs have been lost.

In general, the benefits of belonging to a district are greater for small enterprises. However, the determining factor in belonging to or creating one is the opportunity to access established networks. Promoting cooperation to different levels (suppliers, subcontractors, business leaders) allows large enterprises to effectively outsource part of the production, and thus generate excess levels of productivity, and allows small businesses easier access to economies of scale, resulting in clearly measurable performance benefits. A further benefit of the competitive advantage of districts is the different assessment of business risk: banks tend to assess the solvability of a company considering the context in which the company operates. Being part of an active, vibrant district could generate a positive effect on interest rates applied compared to different territories.

However, when the leading companies are in crisis, small enterprises are the first to pay the price. This was what happened in the Murgia District and was also one of the reasons today, driving around the area, you see a completely different landscape.

Despite some success stories, overall the leading companies based in the Murgia District did not succeed in compensating exports of low-end products (manufactured abroad) with sales of upper-end goods (produced in the district).

In 2008, Nicoletti, Calia and Natuzzi created one task force to have one voice when asking the authorities for help for the entire district. They were hopeful that the leader in the district might be aligned with the task force's position. But, in June 2008, the first giant collapsed.

Nicoletti declared bankruptcy. After 40 years of activity, production stopped. A large proportion of responsibility for this also has to be given to the banks, which decided to freeze the credit limit for Nicoletti as soon as the first warning signals went up.

Calia then bought the Nicoletti brand, creating Nicoletti Trade, a trading company focused solely on the distribution of sofas produced completely by subcontractors.

The dream of Nicoletti and Calia was definitely dead. In October 2008, excluding Natuzzi, the other 1,200 employees were affected by restructuring plans in the district, representing 38% of the total workforce.[96]

In literature, economists attribute the failure of a district to the following: low levels of investment in product innovation and process; lack of skills in financial management; a shortage of specialized professionalism; lack of cooperation among companies; an inability to control the markets; and lack of attention to changes in demand, competition, sometimes even unfair foreign production; and limited support from the local authorities.

---

96   Salotti. Gli operai espulsi salgono a quota tremila, La Gazzetta di Matera, 3 October, 2008.

Many of these factors can be also found in the history of the Murgia District: a myopic view of profit, competition logic based on price, few business leaders and businesses with limited size to grow, a careless political system and the presence of illegal activity.

A deep analysis of the district was done by the Italian economist Ricciardi, focusing on its life cycle stages: Generally, the district's organizational model presented an evolutionary process characterized by three phases: specialization of production, strengthening the relations between enterprises and maturity.

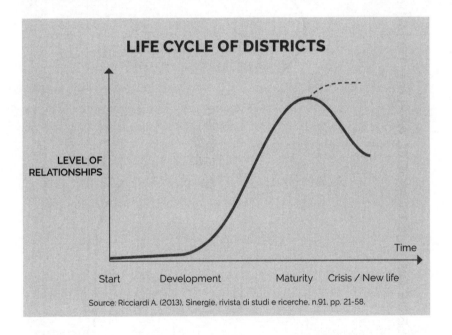

Source: Ricciardi A. (2013), Sinergie, rivista di studi e ricerche, n.91, pp. 21-58.

If we apply this model to the Murgia District, we end up with the following picture.

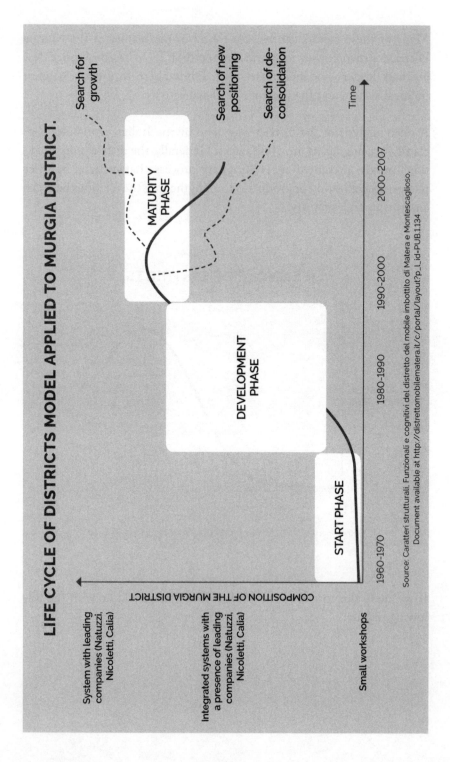

LIFE CYCLE OF DISTRICTS MODEL APPLIED TO MURGIA DISTRICT.

COMPOSITION OF THE MURGIA DISTRICT

System with leading companies (Natuzzi, Nicoletti, Calia)

Integrated systems with a presence of leading companies (Natuzzi, Nicoletti, Calia)

Small workshops

START PHASE

DEVELOPMENT PHASE

MATURITY PHASE

Search for growth

Search of new positioning

Search of de-consolidation

Time

1960-1970 1980-1990 1990-2000 2000-2007

Source: Caratteri strutturali. Funzionali e cognitivi del distretto del mobile imbottito di Matera e Montescaglioso.
Document available at http://distrettomobilematera.it/c/portal/layout?p_l_id=PUB.1134

Natuzzi was the only company that survived the financial and economic tsunami that occurred in the district. This was only possible thanks to Pasquale, who defended the company with all his strength, planned the delocalization, worked together with his main stakeholders to find a way out for his people and insisted on carrying on, despite adversity.

"Working as a team with the other companies in the district would have reduced the number of victims. Other companies had to differentiate their commercial offerings rather than copying Natuzzi's and then offer it at a lower price,"[97] Giuseppe Desantis said.

One of the merits of Natuzzi, from a macroeconomic standpoint, was in the capacity of retaining know-how and expertise that otherwise would have been lost. As such, the company also defended the values of a territory that allowed the district itself to be born.

---

97   Giuseppe Desantis, interview performed in January 2017.

Pasquale Natuzzi during the ceremony at the
American Furniture Hall of Fame, 2008

Natuzzi Store Cairo, Egypt, 2010

The first Natuzzi store in the USA, New York, 2003

Natuzzi Store in Dubai, UAE, 2005

Domino model, 2005

CHAPTER 8
THE YEARS OF REDEMPTION
(2011–2016)

"We must never give up on the challenge of continuous innovation, processes and product development by making sure that the company is streamlined to cope with the obstacles presented by global competition through countries offering cheap labour."[98]

"The long path taken 14 years ago is leading us towards results that we all desire, but the last mile is tough, and we cannot do it alone. We need to feel around us the proximity of the territory, the confidence of the banks, the responsibility of politicians and the affection of the trade unions."[99]

Over 52 years, Natuzzi reinvented itself many times. First, by leveraging the great intuition of its founder, then by scaling up offerings with the addition of affordable products to a bigger consumer base, and then by competing globally against new players from countries with lower costs.

These challenges were quite extensively outlined in the company's 2010 Annual Report:

- External factors:
  - The worldwide economic downturn over the past few years has impacted the group's business and may continue to significantly impact operations, sales, earnings and liquidity in the foreseeable future
  - The group's operations have benefited at times from a temporary workforce reduction program that, if not continued, may have an impact on the group's future performance
  - The group operates in a highly competitive industry that includes a large number of manufacturers. No single company has a dominant position in the industry. Competition is generally based on product quality, brand name recognition, price and service
  - Fluctuations in currency exchange rates have adversely affected the group's results

---

98   Pasquale Natuzzi in 2014, De Santis F., "Gli imprenditori Insieme per combattere la crisi", Gazzetta del Mezzogiorno, 4 December 2014.

99   Pasquale Natuzzi in La Gazzetta del Mezzogiorno, 21 December, 2014.

- ○ To survive in the market, it is key to offer a wide range of products at different price points to attract a wider base of consumers and to continue opening new stores, managing their growth and profitability
- Internal factors:
  - ○ The group's future profitability and financial condition depended on its ability to continue to successfully restructure its operations.

The transformation of Natuzzi into a new company and its ability to plan and control global distribution was a complex process. Equally complex was the repositioning of the brand. Both required profound changes that impacted the production and logistics, distribution strategies and communication, and the managerial structure.

These changes were only possible thanks to the financial resources available due to the reinvestment of profits over the years.

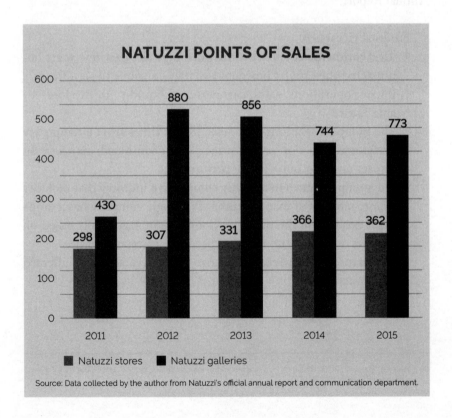

Source: Data collected by the author from Natuzzi's official annual report and communication department.

The key focus of the group was to expand and strengthen its presence in the global upholstered furniture market in terms of sales and production, while at the same time increase the group's profit and efficiency.

The number of stores and galleries continued to grow and reached more than 1,000 worldwide between 2012 and 2015.

To accelerate its strategy, three main aims were explored during this time: increase competitiveness, improve product and enhance the brand.

The Search for Competitiveness

The increase of competitiveness was achieved both inside and outside the production plants. The number of manufacturing sites was reduced, reaching a number of six facilities in Italy in 2012 and three warehouses (one for leather, one for finished goods and one for accessories).

Inside the plants, the group initiated a 'lean production' process review that aimed to improve product quality while regaining competitiveness through more efficient production. By December 2010, new prototypes of a more efficient product line were created.

These new production lines produced approximately 60% of the Italian production of motion products (sofa and armchair with automated motion components embedded). Natuzzi then moved the manufacturing of wooden frames from Santeramo to the Jesce plant, further optimizing productivity and logistics through a direct, in-loco integration of sofa assembly. After this solution had been piloted and shown successful results in the Italian plants, the lean production process was exported to other manufacturing plants abroad.

The Supply Chain Management Department played a key role in the cost-reduction initiative. This department continuously searched for alternative suppliers to continue manufacturing top-quality products at the most competitive prices. Procurement plans were put in place to seek the raw materials and components required using an 'on demand' and 'upon forecast' approach.

The first procurement plan was related to materials and components that required a shorter lead time. This allowed the group to handle a higher number of product combinations (in terms of models, versions and coverings) for customers all over the world, while maintaining a high level of service and minimizing inventory size. Procuring raw materials and components 'on demand' eliminated the risk that these materials and components would become obsolete during the production process.

The second procurement plan – 'upon forecast' – was related to those materials and components that required a long lead time. This plan balanced the group's desire to maintain low inventory levels against the Sales Department's need for flexibility to fulfil orders and maintain customer satisfaction.

Further cost reduction was achieved through the optimization of loads when products were shipped to customers. This load optimization was obtained thanks to software developed through a research partnership with the University of Bari and the University of Copenhagen. The software was used to manage customer orders being shipped by sea, and its goal was to maximize the number of orders shipped through fully loaded containers. If a customer's order did not make optimal use of the space inside a container, revisions to the order quantities were suggested. This activity, which was previously only practiced at the group's headquarters, has since been transferred to Natuzzi Americas and extended to foreign plants.

The group used additional software, developed in partnership with the Polytechnic of Bari and the University of Lecce, to minimize total transportation costs. This software takes into account volume of loads and determines an optimized route to customers in defined areas.

Another lever to be pulled to become competitive was the labour cost. In May 2011, Natuzzi signed a supplementary contract with the unions, in which the company guaranteed contributions of €13,000 for voluntary leave and annual variable incentives for those who increased their productivity.

Then, in September 2011, due to the persistently difficult business environment that had negatively affected the group's order flow, the company renewed the agreement with the Italian trade unions and the Ministry of Labour pursuant to which it was entitled to benefit from an Italian temporary layoff program – 'Cassa Integrazione Guadagni Straordinaria' (CIGS) – for a two-year period.

Between 2011 and 2013 the average number of positions in the CIGS program within the group's Italian facilities was 1,273. On October 2011, the Italian Ministry of Labour accepted the request and admitted Natuzzi to a 24-month layoff period to support the reorganization process of the company.

Unions and employees again began to protest heavily. Although Pasquale had previously announced these layoffs, and asked for State intervention and for mutual cooperation among those involved, the unions did not seem to trust him anymore and asked for a detailed plan on how he planned to relaunch the company. For the first time in the company's history, the white-collar employees of Natuzzi were in the same boat as the blue-collar employees: they all felt abandoned.

Natuzzi was forced to halve its workforce to save the Italian part of the business. Initially, 1,726 layoffs were announced: 1,580 in production and 146 in the offices. This news was a shock for everyone.

The Natuzzi parable seemed to be coming to an end. Ten years earlier, Pasquale had predicted that there would be desertification if the district did not develop infrastructure, if companies did not invest in marketing and branding policies, and if the companies continued with their internal wars rather than teamed up to combat these problems.

"It is the last thing I wanted to do in my business life. But there were no alternatives, and the Chinese competition we have at home is even worse than it is abroad.

"Now I have to secure the company and I have to do everything possible to preserve the work for 2,800 families, but on the condition of being able to revamp ourselves and improve productivity."

The conflict with the unions was very strong: around 400 people were protesting at the entrance of Natuzzi plants every day, stopping any workers from entering

The mediation from the president of the Apulia Region facilitated the dialogue between the company and unions, and the discussion was moved to the table of the Italian government.

A famous episode during this period was 'the revolt led by women'. Tired of the situation, these wise and determined women of Southern Italy decided to do something for their families. These women would stop outside the production plants regularly. But one day they decide to go further and debate with the men who prevented entry into the manufacturing plants and start working again. The general consensus of these women was reported with: *"We will go back to work, we will all work less, but at least we will work. We need to pay our mortgages and cannot afford to wait outside until the situation is sorted out for us."*

During 2013, the framework agreement to support the upholstery district by the Italian government was finally signed, with €101 million allocated to relaunching the manufacturing district in the area. Sixty per cent of this fund came from the local authorities. However, since Natuzzi was laying off its employees, the company itself was not eligible for this program.

So, to get around this, several options were put on the table, including the creation of new companies for Natuzzi's laid-off employees. Through these external companies, they could apply for the grants and state aids and keep going with the production externally. This offered a more flexible and less costly option than if they were to start working at the mother company again anytime soon.

Then, fortunately in October 2013, the company entered into a separate agreement (the 'Italian Reorganization Agreement') that involved a reorganization plan for its Italian operations. The agreement was with local institutions, Italian trade unions, the Ministries of Economic Development and the Ministries of Labour and Social Policy and the region's governing bodies. It also proposed an investment plan over five years that aimed to further develop the Natuzzi Italian brand and safeguard the Italian production. This investment also funded innovation in the company's products, logistics, production processes and staff training.

In terms of the company's workforce, the agreement predicted that the number of redundancies would be reduced from 1,726 employees to 1,506. This was reflected in the company's commitment to the gradual reabsorption of up to 200 manufacturing employees for the production of recliners and up to 20 corporate employees.

Due to the complexity of the measures envisioned by the plan, and to better manage workforce reductions, the company and the trade unions obtained a one-year extension of the company's participation in CIGS. This was due to expire in October 2013, but the extension saw it through October 2014. The company made incentive payments to those who voluntarily resigned, and by end of the period covered by the CIGS program, 600 employees had taken the offer.

Then, in 2014, a new industrial business plan was approved by the board of directors. This plan forecast positive year-end results for 2015 and leveraged a strong recovery of competitiveness in the Italian plants. It was an ambitious plan that relied on the Re-vive armchair and investments in marketing, but also the reduction of warehouses, lean production and the re-engineering of production processes and plants.

From a management standpoint, the company strengthened its structure, with Ernesto Greco coming back at the request of the board of directors, and several other key Italian executives were appointed.

In the meantime, negotiations took place with social parties to obtain a solidarity agreement to help avoid layoffs by reducing working hours for all employees, and reducing labour and social contribution costs.

"We do not want to be laid off. We are losing all hope. What we see is a dark future, no projects, no houses, no children. We want our dignity back, with the help of everyone," Mary Clemente, an employee from the plant in Taranto, told the local press.

'Working less, but work for all' was the new motto.

Finally, in March 2015, the Italian Reorganization Agreement was signed by 95% of employees. This was a fundamental moment for the industrial relaunch of Natuzzi's Italian plants (both from a qualitative and productive standpoint), representing the final step in the production efficiency and work-related cost-reduction processes.

This provided the solidarity agreement the company and the trade unions needed to collaborate and reduce working hours to maintain the company's employment levels during the crisis. The 'Solidarity Agreement' was applicable to 1,918 employees (both blue- and white-collar workers) for a period of 24 months, starting in May 2015.

These 1,918 employees worked reduced hours (on average five hours per day, as opposed to the original eight-hour shifts). This was consistent with the expected order flow that the company foresaw for its Italian productions.

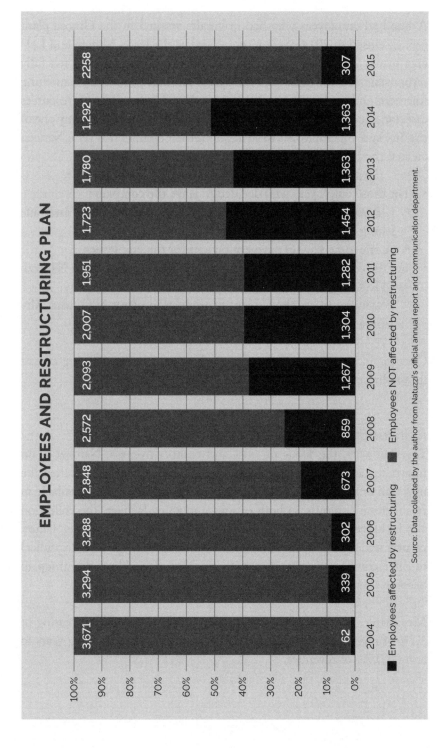

EMPLOYEES AND RESTRUCTURING PLAN

	2004	2005	2006	2007	2008	2009	2010	2011	2012	2013	2014	2015
Employees NOT affected by restructuring	3,671	3,294	3,288	2,848	2,572	2,093	2,007	1,951	1,723	1,780	1,292	2258
Employees affected by restructuring	62	339	302	673	859	1,267	1,304	1,282	1,454	1,363	1,363	307

■ Employees affected by restructuring   ■ Employees NOT affected by restructuring

Source: Data collected by the author from Natuzzi's official annual report and communication department.

A hundred employees who had originally worked in the Ginosa plant (which closed in 2014) were re-employed at the Jesce, Matera and Laterza plants. As for the remaining redundancies, Pasquale still felt fully responsible, like the father of a family. He felt that he must do something for them and, in December 2015, Antonio Cavallera, human resources director, announced the company's determination not to leave any one of the 364 laid-off employees to struggle on their own. In this vein, Natuzzi created the following incentives:

- For those employees who decided to leave the company:
  ○ €40,000 by 31 December 2015, with this figure dropping and vanishing by the end of June 2016;
  ○ A one-time €5,000 payment benefit for the employees
- For the companies that hired employees who decide to leave Natuzzi:
  ○ €12,000 euro, in three annual instalments
  ○ Possibility to use the old empty production plants in Ginosa, Altamura and Santeramo

Once again, this showed how strongly Natuzzi felt about taking care of its employees and helping them until their new careers began.

Reinventing the Products

Together with the focus on cost and competitiveness, Natuzzi again reinvented its products and introduced coffee tables that matched the new wall unit furniture in the Natuzzi collection. These were available in fresh, vibrant colours, in both opaque and shiny lacquer. The collection also included a selection of additional furniture (wall units, tables, lamps, carpets and dining room furniture) and accessories (pots and candles) to offer complete furnishings, with the aim of enabling the group to become a real 'lifestyle company'.

Meanwhile, the company's spending on R&D continued, increasing to 1.7% of revenues in 2013 and then decreasing in the following years to around 0.7% of revenues.

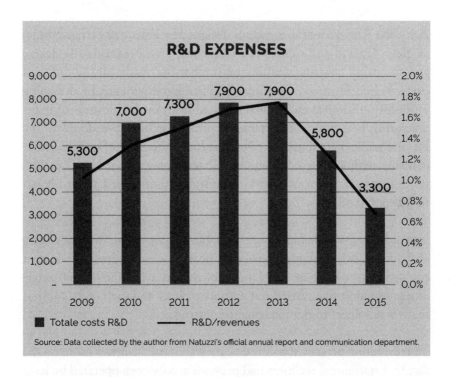

R&D EXPENSES

Source: Data collected by the author from Natuzzi's official annual report and communication department.

Innovation remained a strategic activity for the group and the '3P Project' (Production, Preparation and Process) was put in place. Through the adoption of an innovative methodology specifically for the manufacturing processes, the 3P Project aimed to accomplish goals such as reducing product complexity, improving production efficiency and increasing standardization, and reducing costs.

This project was underway in 2011 and saw the participation of 25 professionals from several departments to discover a new way of designing the products. The objective of the project was to reduce the number of components in armchair models – through a complete re-engineering of the product – and consequently reduce its overall production cost. The project was successful and achieved a 46% reduction in the number of components and a 13% reduction in the production costs of that model.

The results encouraged Natuzzi to extend this methodology to other models of the Softaly collection as well. With an overall investment of €5.2 million, a new product was launched at High Point in October

2013. The Re-vive was an armchair designed by Formway Design Studio of New Zealand and subject to two patents – one covering the design and the other covering the unique mechanism made of 120 different parts. While Formway Furniture had strong experience in designing innovative, technical chairs, Natuzzi had been in the business of manufacturing beautiful, comfortable furniture for over five decades. The Re-vive recliner combined the Natuzzi Italian heritage of quality craftsmanship with leading edge, ergonomic technology from New Zealand. Later that year, the armchair won the Innovation Award at the biggest furniture fair of Paris.[100]

Natuzzi Re-vive armchairs were available in four styles, two sizes (king and queen), two configurations (with or without a headrest), 11 leather colours, four spine/base finishing choices and a coordinated ottoman. The production was carried out entirely in Italy and each of its components was subject to rigorous quality controls.

The revolution presented by the design of this armchair was based on the fact that traditional recliners had previously only been operated by lever mechanisms. Natuzzi designed this product to change that and instead intuitively respond to body movement. Re-vive moves as people move, it flexes as people adjust, providing a seamless transition between body positions. This armchair contributed extensively to order growth in 2014.

In 2015, Natuzzi's range of products included a comprehensive collection of sofas and armchairs with distinguishable styles, coverings and functions that together offered consumers more than 2 million combinations.

From a brand standpoint, the company offered four collections to the market: Natuzzi Italia (upper segment), Natuzzi Re-vive (the iconic product of the Natuzzi Italia collection), Natuzzi Editions collection and the private label collection.

The investment in the brand was still high. During these years, Natuzzi sponsored the World Economic Forum, offered free armchairs to the

---

100 The prize was awarded by a panel of experts during the Furnishing Fair Espritmeuble in Paris.

Petruzzelli Theatre in Bari (for its reconstruction after a fire in 1991), created a special advertising campaign to celebrate the 150-year anniversary of the Italian Republic, sponsored the Italian film festival in London, and launched several photographic exhibitions in their stores.

In 2011, for the first time, according to the World Luxury Tracking Survey by Lagardère Global Advertising, in cooperation with an independent market-research company, IPSOS, the Natuzzi brand was ranked as the best-known global brand within the furniture category, and the second best-known brand overall.

Such recognition of the Natuzzi brand among luxury consumers within the developed world was the result of the huge investments the company had made in its products, communications, in-store experience and customer service, thus securing a premium characteristic in the brand itself.

"What we have communicated is in line with the expectations of luxury consumers," Pasquale Natuzzi said.

This consumer brand awareness encouraged him to carry on with its brand development, by restructuring the group's brand portfolio and enhancing the group's distribution network, to further increase consumers' familiarity with the Natuzzi brand and for it to be recognized as a luxury brand.

Thereafter, Pasquale was no longer simply a craftsman or an entrepreneur. He was acknowledged as a designer, a stylist and an artist.

"At the core of a beautiful object is the perfect balance between creativity, aesthetics and functionality. These requirements must follow a detailed production. But what determines the success of a product is its ability to improve the lives of those who use it," Pasquale declared to a local newspaper in 2013.

But despite all this success, net sales were still decreasing year on year, by thousands of euros. It was only by 2015 that revenues reached the level they had been in 2011.

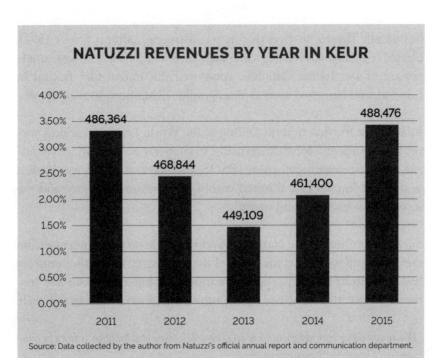

NATUZZI REVENUES BY YEAR IN KEUR

Source: Data collected by the author from Natuzzi's official annual report and communication department.

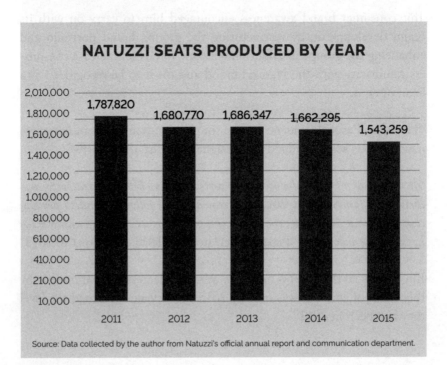

NATUZZI SEATS PRODUCED BY YEAR

Source: Data collected by the author from Natuzzi's official annual report and communication department.

The Heritage of the Murgia District

While the main companies of the Murgia District disappeared, a new phenomenon emerged: the *'Chinesization'* of the manufacturing district.

Chinese entrepreneurs were renting plants in the area from existing subcontractors of these big producers. They were hiring employees on a part-time only basis – four hours a day – but then compelling them to work for 12 hours a day when needed.[101] These practices allowed them to manufacture their products at lower prices than the big competitors. But they were not playing by the same rules: the cost of their production, taxes, salaries, health and safety and social contribution.

A similar phenomenon started to emerge in the north of Italy. The textile district in the Prato area in Tuscany also began to suffer from these practices, devastating the market and altering the rules of healthy competition.

Italian companies like Poltrone & Sofa and Chateau D'Ax were emerging in the market, but their businesses were based on a far simpler model. They designed sofas, but the production was done externally and the majority of their budget was invested in marketing campaigns to promote their brands and sell at low cost.

The main goal of externalized production was to slim manufacturing costs. Tito Di Maggio, president of the Sofa District of Matera and CEO of Sofaland, a company producing sofas for Chateaux d'Ax, declared in several interviews that *"the way subcontractors treat their employees is not my business."* This was an easy way to delegate responsibility to others, although the reality was that the main company was fully aware and responsible for these practices.

Pasquale decided to step up and become the champion of the protest again. It was impossible for any company that was playing by the rules to replicate these activities.

---

101 Souce: Several articles in local newspapers collected by the author

He pushed other companies to denounce such illegality and local authorities made more than 6,000 inspections, which found that 50% of the foreign workers were doing so under illegal conditions.

To make people more aware of this phenomenon, a dedicated advertising campaign was run in all major Italian newspapers. The message was: *"There are sofa discounts, fake 'Made in Italy', black subcontractors, those who practice 'I don't see, I don't know'. And then there are Italians who respect work, laws and people. Next time you buy a sofa, think about it."*

Another ad in 2012 was titled 'Thank you'. This referenced a landmark ruling of Forli court condemning an Italian businessman for the crime of "removal and wilful omission of precautions against accidents at work" where Chinese contractors were working in this vicinity.

In the advertisement below, Natuzzi wanted to thank two entrepreneurs, Elena Ciocca and Manuela Amadori, for their courage in denouncing the irregularities they found to the authorities. Pasquale said, *"There will be no recovery without clean businesses operating in a regime of legality and respect for the rules."*

In 2015, Natuzzi launched a new campaign: 'Not On My Skin'. The key message was that cheap sofas were manufactured at the expense of someone, i.e., those forced to work in poor conditions. *"A sofa with a price too low actually has a high price that we all pay. On our skin."*

It was a shame and an embarrassment that Italian politicians did not seem to care enough at the time to investigate this phenomenon, which posed social and economic risk for the region. Instead, they preferred to pay temporary financial aids, which supported layoffs and delegated action to companies.

Pasquale decided to fight this phenomenon and made moves to involve producers, unions and local authorities in a large-scale organized protest. He was convinced that politicians would be able to detect instances where rules were not being followed by cross-referencing volumes of sales with number of employees, subcontractors and taxes paid.

Pasquale believed that, although this was a laborious exercise, it was one that would generate additional income – in terms of taxes – for the Italian authorities. That year, Pasquale was asked to give a talk at the budget commission at the Italian Chamber of Deputies. Here is a small extract of what he said:

"We believe in recovery, we want to come back and compete, but we cannot do it alone. Entrepreneurs need to be encouraged and helped, we can climb mountains, but we cannot make laws, we cannot change the rules of the game, we cannot reshape economies. These are the tasks for you, that belong to politics, and we welcome these moments of confrontation that can help you draw virtuous paths to revive the fortunes of this country.

"We need to wake up and react; no guarantor has ever saved an employee of a company that fails by unemployment; in the same way, no business owner has ever fired a employee who works seriously and is committed.

"We need to prosecute those entrepreneurs who are not acting in a transparent manner, subcontracting services illegally, producing poor-quality products and placing them on the market at very low prices. Naturally, the large margins of gain in this business model allow many of these companies to invest huge amounts of capital in advertising and promotions, offering products 'Made in Italy', and distorting the market.

"Of course, all this has greatly helped frustrate attempts to action strategies and plans of business development of the authentic and honest entrepreneurs who have put their savings into their companies, often exposing themselves to bankruptcy.

"We are all called to defend companies like Natuzzi, now defined as a bastion of the south with an Italian heritage to defend. Your task, dear politicians, will be to pursue these phenomena for the dignity of all the areas devastated by the crisis, with appropriate laws, which we ourselves will strive to suggest and promote, and so we ask for your invaluable contribution.

"If Italian manufacturing can no longer compete with the workforce in emerging countries, we cannot allow 'Made in Italy' to die, the last bastion of our national economy. It has given so much and has much still to give to this nation, as long as you really want it."

Some companies claimed to produce their products at €0.25 per minute,[102] which was significantly less than the legal salary recommendations for manufacturing employees and the associated taxes. Taking these factors into consideration, the minimum salary offered by any company should have been €0.41 per minute.

Pasquale had serious doubts about the ways in which such companies, including those driving the sofa district association in Matera, worked. He argued that the majority of these companies were only able to reduce their costs because they chose to lay off their employees and employ subcontractors who worked in illegal conditions and set ups.

In comparison to these, Natuzzi reported a cost per minute of €0.68, substantially higher than the minimum. But it was also impossible to produce the standard, design and quality of Natuzzi products at a lower price.

During these years, the district established a body that would create a code of ethics and a permanent office to monitor the situation in the market. The response from the president, Tito Di Maggio, to Pasquale and other critics was very poor. And there was a conflict of interest that existed – which everyone concerned was aware of – that the president of the sofa district was also the CEO of Sofaland, the main company acting in this way.

The banking system also played a role in this crisis. Rather than supporting local economies with financing projects to promote the situation, they decided to close the credit lines.

Despite everything, Pasquale believed that companies could only survive such a crisis with determination, strength, ethical behaviour, and respect for integrity, customers and stakeholders.

At this point, in 2015 the company claimed the statement 'Natuzzi. Harmony Makers," which resonated with the image they were creating

---

102 Carlo Puca, *"La guerra delle Poltrone"*, Panorama, 17 July, 2013.

of themselves. Solidarity agreements with the unions meant that the majority of employees stayed with the company, and a new project named ASSIST helped drive the company forward. This involved three pillars:

- Brand innovation: focus the competition on the customer experience
- Process and product innovation: continue driving innovation in the sector and develop new products to create or satisfy customer's needs
- Lean production: in all plants

These pillars would be enough to ensure the growth and the continuation of Natuzzi's success in years to come. Looking back at the story of Natuzzi, the company was definitely a different one at this stage.

Pasquale Natuzzi receives the 'Lifetime Achievement' award from the
League Against Defamation, 2011

The Italian President of the Republic, Sergio Mattarella visits the Natuzzi
booth at the Salone del Mobile in Milan, 2017

Cover of the *Word Excellence* financial magazine dedicated to
Pasquale Natuzzi on ethics and business

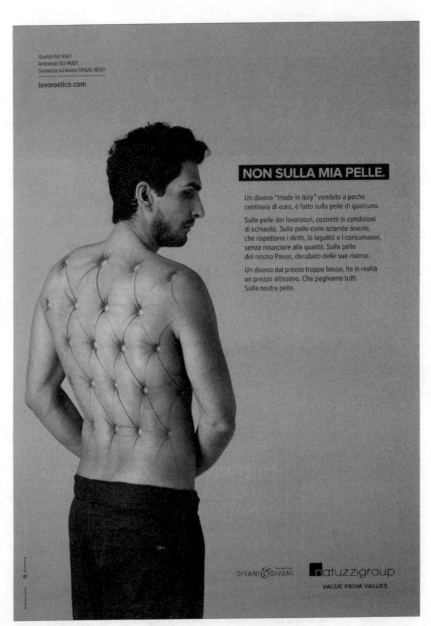

'Not on My Skin' campaign

RE-VIVE, the first performance recliner that reacts intuitively to body movements

Pasquale Natuzzi at work in the Style Center

Natuzzi Italia, Long Beach model, 2015

Natuzzi Italia, Philo model, 2016

CHAPTER 9

CORPORATE SOCIAL RESPONSIBILITY

– THE COLOURS OF BUTTERFLIES

"During one of my many trips to America, I was sitting on the plane next to an old man, his features clearly Asian. He was one of those people who, while not knowing it, immediately instiled confidence.

"I told him about my work, I mentioned briefly my story as an entrepreneur. He listened in silence, and I remember exactly the words that he told me: 'Dear sir, the love and enthusiasm you put into your work are too great to invest in a little thing like profit. I think there is much more to motivate you. And it is not the power.' I asked him the reason for such surety and he replied, 'Power has the colour of the mice, you have the colours of the butterflies.'"[103]

It is clear when looking at Natuzzi how Pasquale has shaped the company in every single way. What is also clear is that, since the very beginning, the company was perceived not just as a business, but as a social asset, made by people and for the people working in it.

The concept of Corporate Social Responsibility (CSR) has always been strongly embedded into the company's way of working. Natuzzi has not exploited its full potential when it comes to promoting its products or as a lever for competitive advantage; instead, sustainability and stakeholder satisfaction are ideas embedded in Natuzzi's DNA.

Italian economist Sciarelli[104] developed the following theory about CSR.

According to the 'social success' theory, in the case of a company where ownership and management coincide with the same person, they transpose much of themselves into the company and the reasons or purposes that motivate them in driving the success of the company can be framed, with any necessary adaptation, according to the famous scale of needs theorized by Maslow.[105]

---

103 Pasquale Natuzzi in Crescere Insieme, 9/1994.

104 Sciarelli S. (1996), "Etica aziendale e finalità imprenditoriali", Economia&Management, n. 6, pp.13-30.

105 Maslow A. (1954) , *Motivation and Personality*, 1954, Harper, New York.

The entrepreneur, therefore, owner and manager, would have these three purposes:

- Keeping the company afloat (with the pursuit of profit)
- Establish itself in the field of social class
- Assume a position of prestige in the community where it operates

These objectives can be seen as goals that are realized in the course of the life of a business.

A businessperson's first goal is to become profitable and to generate revenues to pay back the resources invested in the company. As this profit becomes stable, assuring continuity and harmony in management, he will want to expand presence in the territory and, therefore, perhaps open new stores, using the experience gained with the first one, and try to become the primary chain of stores in the area the business is operating in.

As time passes by, having steadily achieved profit targets and market power, he will tend to add additional needs, such as to be recognized as the entrepreneur who created jobs, who brought prosperity and the like, so he will search for social prestige, namely recognition by the community where he operates.

Placing these needs in a scale of ethical and economic business purposes proposed by Sciarelli (illustrated in the following picture), it is clear to see that the ethical component increases while the economic one declines or remains stable..

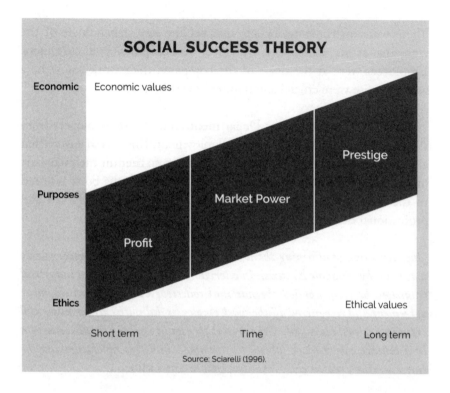

Source: Sciarelli (1996).

The beauty of this model is that the three objectives do not exclude each other, but are integrated.

The social theory model works when the owner is also the one who manages the company.

Going back to Natuzzi's approach to CSR, it is easy to see how Pasquale challenged the social success theory. At Natuzzi, the focus was on profits only in the early stages; soon after, this shifted to three main pillars:[106]

- *Be a development hub for the whole territory*
- *Be a source of employment and income*
- *Act as the culture engine for employees and citizens of the district within which we operate*

---

106 Crescere Insieme, vol 13-14/95, page 4.

These were instrumental beliefs that set the key stakeholders of the company as its employees, the local communities and customers. Employees were at the heart of the company; their work, know-how and expertise were crucial and matured over the years.

Natuzzi's Human Resources Department took care of employees from the very first day they started their employment. This was to ensure that employees reached their full potential, but also so that they felt like part of the family. All those who were interviewed for this book referred to the time they worked at Natuzzi as a great time of personal and professional experience.

"The revolution of affirming the workers rights in this area of southern Italy was made by Pasquale Natuzzi. In a territory with a very limited industrial tradition, he from applied the national collective bargaining employment agreement and recognized all the work employees did with extra bonuses and extra incentives. He established a respect for legality among small workshops in a context where black labour was common and this revolutionized the entire territory positively,"[107] Giuseppe Desantis said.

As far back as 1994, internal education training had been established to boost the performance and knowledge of Natuzzi's workforce. By creating the Natuzzi Corporate University, the company trained local individuals for professions that they would hold in the years to come. Some of the individuals receiving training would have been hired by Natuzzi itself, while others would find jobs in other companies. The university benefited both the company and the employees, and at the same time generated positivity in the local communities.

Christmas parties, the company library, social events and the in-house magazine all played a vital role in creating a virtual and cohesive community, while transmitting the core values of the company and high attention to productivity, quality and efficiency.

Such consideration towards their employees led Natuzzi to win the Sinergia Award[109] in 1995 as recognition of *"the central key role of human resources and the development in place to move from a family business to a professional one."*

Outside the workplace, employees continued to feel the presence of Natuzzi in their lives, since the company organized social activities, discounts in local shops, soccer tournaments, holiday packages at low prices and so on.

Local communities also developed a close relationship with the company, since it presented hope for the local population in a difficult macroeconomic environment. At that time, there were approximately 27,000 inhabitants in the village of Santeramo in Colle. The area's economy – agriculture, knitting and craft shops – came to rely exclusively on Natuzzi, which over the years provided an endless source of employment.

Due to this strong connection with the village, in 1993 Pasquale became involved in the city council to identify and share with the local authorities the company's requirements for growth. This involved the rehabilitation of roads, construction of car parks and expansion of the water network.

"Growing means to collaborate and work together; it means designing together and speeding up processes that allow a healthy development for all, both for the company and for the country." This was the message that Natuzzi wanted to launch in this town.

Partnerships with local universities were also established. These activities of solidarity and philanthropy showed an understanding of the local communities. For instance, the company gave financial support to restructure a historical UNESCO heritage area – Sassi in Matera, in particular the Palace San Pietro Barisano development – into a location to host cultural events and entertainment.

These were years when the company's mission was *"to increase the well-being and improve the quality of life, spreading in its territory a new and advanced culture of progress through the productive activities.*

---

107 Giuseppe Desantis, interview performed in January 2017.

108 The Sinergia Award is an Italian prestigious recognition of the Italian Association of Human Resources Directors aimed at recognizing the value of the best Human Resources management program across companies.

"Pasquale Natuzzi's dream was to employee around 4,000 people in Apulia, and each one of us was working for this social mission," employees recalled in an interview.[109]

"He has the credit of having discovered the talents of the region, making them grow and develop. Murgia is an area where the soil is barren, full of stones, and people are used to having to roll up their sleeves and work a small piece of land in order to survive. This attitude towards sacrifice, towards working as a team with great passion and being guided by the 'values' of Pasquale Natuzzi, has improved the socioeconomic context in which it works

"The best motto was: I work, I create work.

"The sense of pride has, for many years, created an element of great cohesion and strength due to the fact that many men and women are committed to creating success,"[110] Giuseppe Desantis recalled.

Another key stakeholder of Natuzzi has always been its customers, the reason for the company's existence.

Natuzzi is a market-centric company, where the markets dictate their needs and preferences and the management translates these into collections of furniture. Since the beginning, Natuzzi's attention to detail, high quality standards, and taylorism in production have been the key drivers of its relationship with customers.

Natuzzi has always considered quality to be a wide concept that also involves suppliers, by ensuring that the quality of services/goods provided by them are sufficient to maintain high quality in the final product. This approach encourages a company culture, a partnership with commercial partners, rather than merely external companies providing raw materials.

Through this partnership, Natuzzi has had a positive influence on its suppliers' way of working. Natuzzi has been able to increase its partners' standards by enabling them to work in a safer environment and understand and respect legality in an economy where the State is sometimes more of a hindrance than a help.

Quality of production was also ensured through the continuous improvement of the mechanism in place at the production sites. Production of leather sofas requires chemical agents and, to safeguard against harm to the local environment, an internal department was put in place to measure water quality and ensure a depuration procedure was in place.

Another important stakeholder group was the shareholder community. Pasquale is not a 'yes man', and he is not afraid to show the way he likes to drive the company.

He knew that the company's listing on the New York Stock Exchange was a big opportunity for the company, since it provided the opportunity to access financial resources. At the same time, he knew that being listed would drive the maturity of the company and obligate managers to consider the bottom line. Over the years, the dividend policy was very conservative and, as the company's equity grew, this provided a clear direction for management to reinvest the positive net income into the future development of the company.

The market was also a key stakeholder; the market was where Natuzzi drew inspiration and fought the battle for growth and endurance. On many occasions Pasquale emphasized the importance of his connection to the territory: *"Usually I like to think of my company as a large tree with roots firmly in Southern Italy and branches worldwide. The place where I live and work – between Apulia and Basilicata – is fascinating and full of history and art. A welcoming land where time seems to stand still, having found refuge here and hospitality. I am fascinated by our wonderful hills with almond and olive trees. Our products are the fruits of the special feeling between our work and our land: the colours, the climate, the Mediterranean are the sources of our inspiration, along with the happy multicultural influences of a global group like ours, where people of different cultures and traditions work together."*[111]

---

109 Pietro Lascaro and Gianmichele Pace, interviews performed in January 2017.

110 Giuseppe Desantis interview performed in January 2017.

111 Pasquale Natuzzi in Interni, 2013, page 444.

Though Natuzzi's original focus was customers, suppliers, environment and local communities, soon after employees and subcontractors became the core of the CSR approach.

On many occasions, Pasquale would encourage employees to be proud of their work, their expertise and their know-how. But, at the same time, the illegal subcontractors, producing identical products at a much lower cost, were putting the work that Natuzzi had done over the years at risk.

During the years of big crisis, Natuzzi CSR focused on these two categories:

• The employees, which included several interventions, starting from converting the indirect workers to direct, asking local banks to guarantee employee loans for the purchase of their first homes, investing in education, marketing and brand awareness to increase sales and therefore to maintain employment of employees
• The subcontractors and the local authorities, raising the awareness of the phenomenon. Dedicated campaigns in national newspapers, discussions in the Italian parliament, and participations in TV shows.

In this turbulent period, Pasquale felt the need to steer and strengthen the organization through the definition of new corporate values and a style of management adequate for this change.[112] This ensured that all key stakeholders were focused on the same target in mind: the relaunch of the company. The key stakeholders that reflected these values included employees, customers, shareholders, and commercial partners.

The first attempt to revise the corporate values was in 2008 with the 'colonization model'. Top management, together with an external consulting agency, worked out the definition of the company values. The level of engagement was high, the output exciting, but the set of values were too alien to the company because they came from an external creative process instead of stemming from Natuzzi Group's own history and corporate authentic identity.

---

112 Mazzei A., Quarantino L. (2011), *Looking for the roots of future success: corporate values to drive organizational change in Natuzzi* Group, Conference on Corporate Communication June 7, 2011.

A new attempt in 2010 was called the 'enhancement model'. In this model, top management used the company's existing best practices, by looking at its past, to define how the company would like to be in the future.

These new values focused on two key words: responsibility and accountability. They impacted the company and stakeholders in various ways, including:

- For customers – listening to them and seeking their happiness through a unique shopping experience, excellent products, and innovative services in line with their expectations.
- For commercial partners – establishing sincere relationships in terms of legality, transparency and always in the interest of customers.
- For shareholders – demonstrating the economic success of the company through the judicious use of resources, the continuous search for innovative solutions and market opportunities.
- For employees – respecting them to enhance and to upgrade their professionalism, encouraging opportunities for integration between different countries and cultures.
- For society – a sense a duty to work for the good of the territories, respecting the environment and combining social solidarity with economic sustainability.

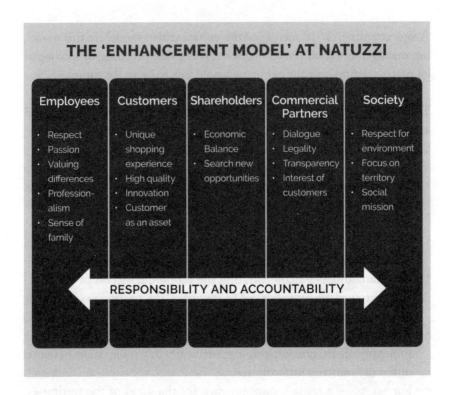

These values then became the 'bible' for Natuzzi managers. And by looking at Natuzzi today, it is easy to track how these values have translated into practices in all Natuzzi's operations.

Employees

For example, although Natuzzi had ensured that its high standards were applied to its production sites in China, Brazil and Romania, when the new plant in Shanghai was opened, the situation was not great. Antonio Ventricelli recalled in an interview: *"Buildings without air conditioning and without heating systems, where people worked in -6 degrees Celsius, benches that were only 20 centimetres above the ground, seamstresses who were seated on stools made of foam, carpentry sections were filled with a mountain of sawdust and the tools used were not professional.*

"We have revolutionized these working conditions ... We have changed the layout of plants ... We slowly created a revolution for the people working there.

This was recognized by the workers and, on the day we opened the doors to employ new staff, we found 300–400 people who wanted to work for us queuing outside the plant."[113]

Society

Another example that demonstrates the dedication of Natuzzi to these values was seen in 2011. The United Nations declared 2011 as the International Year of Forests, so the company decided to focus on further improving the governance in place for the protection and enhancement of trees and forests.

Wood is a key material for production and, from a CSR standpoint, it is important to ensure that wood is legally produced and comes from forests managed in a responsible manner. The Natuzzi Group makes a conscious effort to not purchase or accept wood illegally extracted from unchecked and endangered forests. In fact, before any wood stock is purchased, even its derivatives, the Natuzzi team collects the data required to prove the source is ethical.

The Natuzzi Group takes this very seriously and has measures to break relationships with suppliers who:

- Cannot provide appropriate documents that declare the country of origin and confirm the legal status of the wood stock, the exact position the tree was cut and transportation. The seller is committed to providing these documents to the buyer within 48 hours upon request
- Are funded to provide wood from intact natural forests or other sites geographically identified as 'High Conservation Value Forests'
- Sell wood that is sourced from forests related to social conflicts, from logging operations in tropical or subtropical regions linked to the project of converting natural forests to plantations, and wood originated from genetically modified trees.

---

113 Antonio Ventricelli, interview performed in January 2017.

Due to its continued high diligence in this area, Natuzzi received the Forest Stewardship Council's (FSC) Chain-of-Custody certification in 2016. This badge shows consumers that the wooden material used in Natuzzi's products comes from well-managed forests, respecting the social, economic and environmental needs of present and future generations.

In addition to monitoring wood suppliers, the company also takes care to ensure all raw materials are ethical and environmentally friendly. This includes:

- Source of polyurethane – this is produced by IMPE, an ISO 140001-certified company. These are a set of environmental standards that help organizations manage production with minimal impact on the environment, while complying with applicable laws, regulations and other environmentally oriented requirements.
- Using 21,000 UV panels installed on the rooftops of Natuzzi plants and trading offices. This system ensures an annual reduction of approximately 3,400 tonnes in CO^2 emissions, equal to that of the annual emission of about 1,200 cars.

Natuzzi is also focused on raising the awareness around energy consumption:

- In Natuzzi's Romanian plant, 52% of energy consumed comes from renewable sources, and waste from wood processing is used as thermal power, providing 78% of the energy required to heat the production facility[115]
- In Italy, the headquarters and all Divani&Divani shops participate in an awareness campaign about energy saving and sustainable lifestyles
- In Brazil, the company is currently investigating the option of installing a glass roof that could potentially reduce energy used for lighting
- In China, a new pilot system is in place to collect waste from wood production and transform them into pellets, usable for heating.

---

115 Source: 2015 Sustainability Report Natuzzi.

Perhaps the main raw material used by Natuzzi is leather, which the group ensures is sourced from cattle bred to become part of the food chain. The mantle is recovered, processed and transformed by a company named Natco (Pozzuolo, Friuli), the group's tannery. Large investments have been made in R&D to use more environmentally friendly tanning products. The white leather, for example, thanks to an innovative tanning process, does not use of chromium and other heavy metals. Natco has been certified an ISO 14001 environmental system.

Another important raw material used are feathers for padding, and Natuzzi only purchases these from suppliers who respect animals and the quality standards. In particular, the suppliers must:

* Monitor and verify the working process (the former EC Regulation 1069/2009)
* Adhere to the code of conduct that condemns any practice of defeathering from live animals, as required by the traceability standard EDFA, and are in possession of the traceability certificate.

When it comes to contribution to local communities, the company used its power and influence in the territory in a key project called 'Open Art'. This idea was introduced through a collaboration with Arnaldo Pomodoro from the Salone Del Mobile furniture fair in Milan. The project became official in April 2009, with the goal to bring art into Natuzzi stores and make it accessible to everyone.

Natuzzi Open Art allows collaboration with contemporary artists from all backgrounds to create site-specific works of art that are displayed in Natuzzi's flagship stores around the world. The first collaboration was with sculptor Giacomo Benevelli, followed by partnerships with Nicola De Verme and Gianni Basso. The latest project, in December 2015, saw French artist Adrien Missika create an art installation at the Natuzzi Store in Miami.

Another contribution to the wider society, together with Italian entrepreneur Nicola Benedetto, was the construction of the first 'House for Peace', a project dedicated to the reception of refugees, in the south of Italy. 'House of Peace' was replicated in areas where the reception of refugees is a structural phenomenon. The building is shaped like the wings of a butterfly and uses innovative technologies for saving energy.

In reference to this, Pasquale said: *"Being hospitable does not mean only making our customers' homes harmonious and comfortable, as we do every day through our work. Being hospitable also means rolling up our sleeves to defend the right of everyone to have shelter, when they are on the run from war and famine. This is the reason Natuzzi supports the City of Peace Foundation."*

There is still a long way to go to reach 'best in class' when it comes to CSR, leveraging it to empower the brand and embed the company's value fully into the brand proposition.

But the company is fully committed to sustainability. *"Our commitment for sustainable development is not only a responsibility, but also an opportunity. It expresses a forward-looking investment that is fundamental to every company's continuity. Renewable energies are also an opportunity to compete, keeping the operating costs low. Combining the sustainable development with the competition is a challenge that our company wants to carry on to improve the quality of life in the territory,"* said Pasquale.

Pasquale's passion and determination will certainly allow the company to make his desires more visible to the external world.

Natuzzi Italia Store, Taipei, Taiwan

CHAPTER 10

WHAT IS BEHIND A SOFA?

"We know there is something else to our success. It is something that does not belong to the culture and way of working of the others, including the finance world. As we wrote on the cover of our annual report: 'the love for our work has made us the great craftsmen in the world.'

"What is love for work? It is the chopper who stretches the leather on the table, who caresses it before cutting, to discover the most invisible defects. It is the seamstress who opens her eyes to make a straight line. It is the assembler hugging pillows, dressing them to give them shape. And it is Giovanni, Salvino, Nicola, Orsola, and Antonio, who spend their Sundays in the prototype room making the latest model the most beautiful and the most comfortable it can be. This is a love that our competitors do not have. And this love allows us to look at the future with greater confidence. Others would not understand, even if we said it. And maybe they would not even believe. But we do not care. Because we know that without our great love for the job, we would have gotten nowhere."[116]

The production of upholstered furniture is labour intensive and can be split into five main steps, as shown in the picture below.

---

116 Introduction speech at the University of Bari, 2001, for the conferral of the honorary degree to Pasquale Natuzzi.

TYPICAL UPHOLSTERED PRODUCTION CYCLE

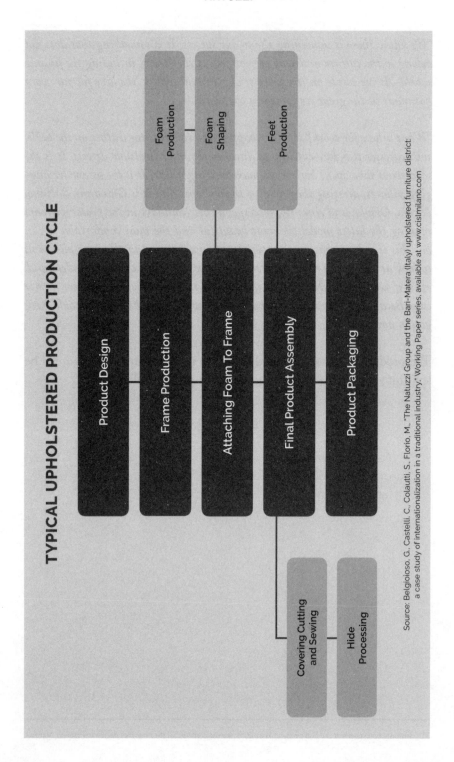

Source: Belgioioso, G., Castelli, C., Colautti, S., Florio, M., "The Natuzzi Group and the Bari-Matera (Italy) upholstered furniture district: a case study of internationalization in a traditional industry." Working Paper series, available at www.cislmilano.com

The first step for each company is to define which product to produce, with the design phase. Once the design is complete, the sofa frame is produced, either in wood or in iron.[117]

The next step is to produce and shape the polyurethane foam, used for filling. It is usually supplied by external manufacturers, as it requires huge investments, while the foam shaping is often performed by sub-suppliers.

Once the foam is shaped and the frame is ready, the next step is to attach the foam to the frame. This process too is often decentralized, since the contribution to the added value of the product is low.

The hide processing (including several steps, such as tanning, colouring, softening and drying to get the final leather finish) is often performed by sub-suppliers.

Different approaches are required for the cutting and sewing phases, depending on whether the sofa has a leather or a textile covering. This is a crucial phase that affects the quality and the final cost of the product and requires great skill. Therefore, companies tend to control this phase of the production internally, especially for high quality upholstered sofas.

If we look at Natuzzi's process of developing and producing a sofa, we end up with the following picture. You can immediately see the complexity around it, compared to an 'ordinary production process'.

---

117 The process described here is presented by Belgioioso, G., Castelli, C., Colautti, S., Florio, M., "The Natuzzi Group and the Bari-Matera (Italy) upholstered furniture district: a case study of internationalization in a traditional industry," Working Paper series, available at www.cislmilano.com

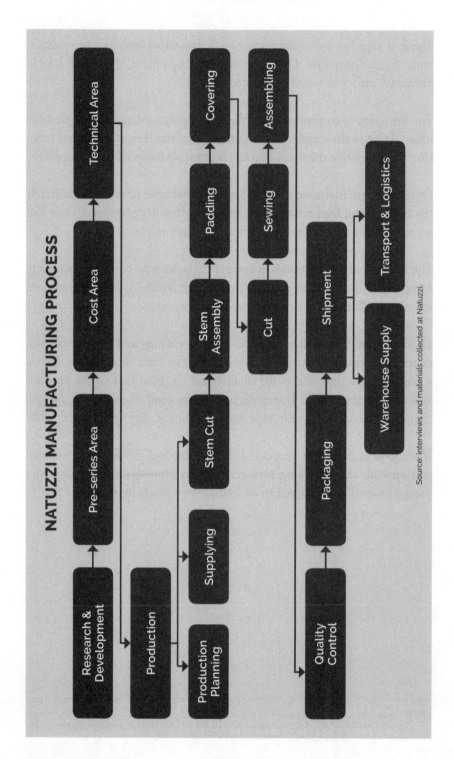

NATUZZI MANUFACTURING PROCESS

Research & Development → Pre-series Area → Cost Area → Technical Area

Production → Production Planning → Supplying → Stem Cut → Stem Assembly → Padding → Covering

Cut → Sewing → Assembling

Quality Control → Packaging → Shipment → Warehouse Supply → Transport & Logistics

Source: interviews and materials collected at Natuzzi.

The main differences are in the preproduction phase:

- Strong importance of the R&D department, where new trends are detected and new products are studied, designed and invented. This area has the role and responsibility of sensing the market, identifying and interpreting customer needs and tastes to create prototypes;
- Existence of a mini-plan for simulation (pre-series area). This is a factory in miniature with two main aims: to determine the average time to execute the production and to measure quantity of materials needed to produce each single product;
- Existence of a cost area, where an assessment is performed on how much the product could cost;
- A technical office, responsible for creating designs.

There is still a lot of dexterity in the work performed by artisans at Natuzzi. When they translate designs into a piece of furniture, the key peculiarity of the production process is the willingness to industrialize an artisanal production.

One of the first challenges was implementing the 'just-in-time' methodology. This is an inventory strategy companies employ to increase efficiency and decrease waste by receiving goods only as they are needed in the production process, thereby reducing inventory costs. This method requires producers to forecast demand accurately.[118]

This technique has several advantages over traditional models. Production runs remain short, which means manufacturers can move from one type of product to another very easily. This method reduces costs by eliminating warehouse storage needs. Companies also spend less money on raw materials because they buy just enough to make the products and no more.

Among the several disadvantages is the disruption to the supply chain. If a supplier of raw materials has a breakdown and cannot deliver the goods on time, one supplier can shut down the entire production process.

---

118 Definition of Investopedia, available at http://www.investopedia.com/terms/j/jit.asp

A sudden order for goods that exceeds expectations may delay the delivery of finished products to clients.

At first, Natuzzi tried to automate the inventories, since goods used for upholstery production can require lot of space. In the 90s, Natuzzi created automatic warehouses with trans-elevators selecting and moving products. Leather or textiles, after sewing, were stored in boxes and put in stock by automatic systems. Rigid connections move goods along the production line or automatic guided vehicles (AGVs) were used.

Through the just-in-time strategy, Natuzzi was able to reduce its stock and increase the speed of execution of an order from six weeks to only four weeks.

Another topic was subcontractors. Initially Natuzzi was managing part of the production leveraging on external companies to produce foam, frames, and other components. All these companies were located in different areas, and the target was to develop a system to ensure that the material arrived shortly before its use.

Many of those companies were family-based, and the mindset change required was tough in many cases.

Pietro Lascaro, production engineer at Natuzzi, recalled, *"Internet connections were nonexistent. We had to bring to subcontractors the telephone lines, the terminals, the modems at our expense and install software that created the bill of material simultaneously in the suppliers' ERP and that of Natuzzi's, so the production plants could know a couple hours in advance which goods were coming in."*[119]

But to guarantee quality, speed and volumes, this was not enough. Natuzzi decided to control part of the production: a carpentry shop was created, a company producing polyurethane bought (IMPE) and a dedicated company created to shape the polyurethane (Natex).

Pasquale is a strong believer in automation and the power of information technology. And from the very beginning, craftsmen and technology coexisted in Natuzzi's production plants.

Process automation was considered a key value for the whole company.

"We equipped every sewing station with a personal computer where the operator, simply inputting the product ID, could see on the screen which model they were producing, the specifics of the product and also the CAD designs to ensure a professional, high-quality execution of the work," said Gianni Romaniello.

"On average we had 400 models and to teach all of them in a classroom was not practical. We found the best way was to give the operator the option to learn how to execute the model by doing.

"The software also calculated the lead time of each operator, to monitor performance and eventually correct the standard costs and times. Through this mechanism we made the technical specification of a product, initially difficult to understand, accessible to every single operator, even without engineering or technical knowledge.

"Having production shifts with more than 800 operators, it was very hard for the manager of the plant to distribute the work around all of the people. We created software with the University of Lecce that, based on the production history of each operator, could assign models according to the complexity and the experience of the people, to speed up the execution of the product."[120]

In carpentry, pantographs were applied to speed up the production of drums. Machines for the automatic filling of the cushions were also designed.

A key innovation was the application of machines to cut the leather. This is an extremely complicated process, since leather is the most expensive part of a sofa and the most irregular one.

For many years, this step in production was a manual one. This involved an operator placing a mantle of leather on the table and using pieces of wood in the shape of various sofa components to create the different pieces, cutting them with a knife, one by one.

---

119 Pietro Lascaro, interview performed in January 2017.
120 Gianni Romaniello, interview performed in January 2017.

This is a very delicate step, since before cutting the operator must scan the leather and identify qualitative differences (i.e. scars, irregular callus, insect bites) or defects. Based on this analysis, the operator then decides if these features must be avoided or can be inserted into parts of the sofa not visible to the consumer. In this way, the operator can reduce the cost of the leather not used.

In 2009, a revolution was made in this activity by introducing automatic cutting machines, mainly in Italian production plants. With this new approach, the operator was still in control in defining where the leather was to be cut, but the difference was that projectors would highlight virtual shapes on the leather. The operator then decides where to place them with the same logic of the process mentioned above. Once the position of the shapes is finalized, the machine begins to cut the leather. With this new approach, the role of the operator continues to exist, but the cutting activity is completely automated.

A second revolution came from the 'Gemini project', developed in 2016, collaboration with Gemini Cad Systems, a leading global supplier of technology specialized into advanced technologies to automate the manufacturing process from design to cutting. The difference in this approach is that the operator identifies and marks with a special marker the defects of the leather. The machine developed by the project, using a camera and projectors, through a complex calculation of combination of shapes and sizes, decides where to cut in order to optimize the leather usage, but also to optimize the quality of the leather in each single piece. With this development, both the cutting and the other manual activities of nesting were automated.

This project is, without a doubt, very innovative. No other sofa producers in the world use this technology. A similar processes exist in the automotive industry, with the difference that the leather used to produce car seats usually has fewer defects and so the decision on where to cut is easier.

The benefits of this automation are huge. Natuzzi calculated a reduction in the time to produce a sofa by 20%, but also a reduction in leather scrap equivalent to around 1.5 million euros per year.

In addition to these benefits, the automatic scanning of leather also helped improve the supply chain part of the process. This meant that the quality of raw material purchased could be automatically checked and any issues identified could be shared with the vendors immediately.

However, this is not enough at Natuzzi. The company is now working on the next step in innovation, which will consist of creating a machine that has the ability to identify defects automatically and differentiate between those that can be avoided and those that will affect the production process.

Many of these innovations were developed based on suggestions from the operators directly involved in the production process or employees in the R&D department.

"The level of automation in Natuzzi and the extreme use of computers had no rival in the district. Other companies were watching Natuzzi as they tried to copy or learn from its production techniques. Natuzzi was the benchmark, the point of reference in the area. The majority of companies in the Murgia District were in a state of evolved craftsmanship, but they could not be regarded as industrialized,"[121] said Pietro Lascaro.

"The complexity of Natuzzi production stands in the need to have the same product all around the world. Ideally, if we split a sofa in all its components and we produce them in different areas, they should come assembled exactly as if they had been produced in the same plant,"[122] said Antonio Cavallera.

Even during the crisis period, Natuzzi never stopped innovating. Pasquale has always seen innovation as a way to reduce indirect activities and stay focused on those that create value for the customer.

Customers are a key asset for Pasquale, and the main goal in all attempts to improve the production process has been to stay focused on the customer and spend time and money on what the customer wants.

---

121 Pietro Lascaro, interview performed in January 2017.
122 Antiono Cavallera, interview performed in February 2017.

Information systems have played a key role in this.

The geographic distribution of sites forced the company to create its own data network to exchange information across plants as early as 1991. This enabled the company to consolidate all the information in a dashboard, where all agents were able to follow their orders and understand at which stage of the production they were. Information and data regarding production were aggregated to allow Pasquale visibility on the efficiency of every plant.

To fully understand what goes into a Natuzzi sofa, we should look at how the production was executed in the past compared to today. In the past, every plant was specialized for a particular step of the production. Once a step was completed, the semi-finished good was boxed and moved to the inventory, awaiting transportation to the next step of the production.

This process brings with it a number of disadvantages, primarily related to the management of warehouses and then to the silos of management in each department. The industrial structure of the group presents the interconnections between departments that involve higher costs and resolution times.

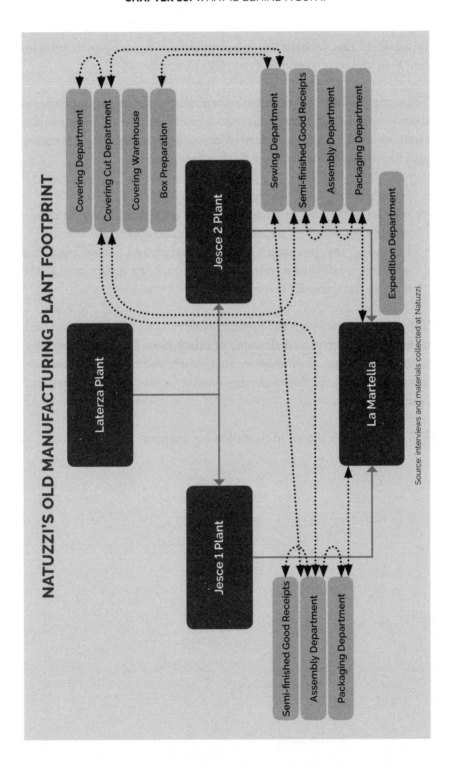

NATUZZI'S OLD MANUFACTURING PLANT FOOTPRINT

Source: interviews and materials collected at Natuzzi.

Based on all this, in 2010 the company decided to innovate its production lines and move towards lean production systems.

Following the Toyota Productive System, analysing the design of its production systems and taking into consideration experiences of companies from other industries, an industrial design project took shape with the goal to review production flows for the benefit of:

- Reduction in product costs, which means gain in margins
- Increasing the level of quality of the products (with a drastic reduction of complaints in today's values of millions of euro)
- Increasing the production speed and eliminate non-value-added activities means guaranteeing each operator the ability to produce more in the space of his work shift

The idea was to redesign the production plants and make sure that each of them directly managed all stages of production. The production plant assumes the shape of production lines, where materials are moved and assembled along the line, reducing time to move materials from one plant to the next.

The new set-up is shown in the following diagram.

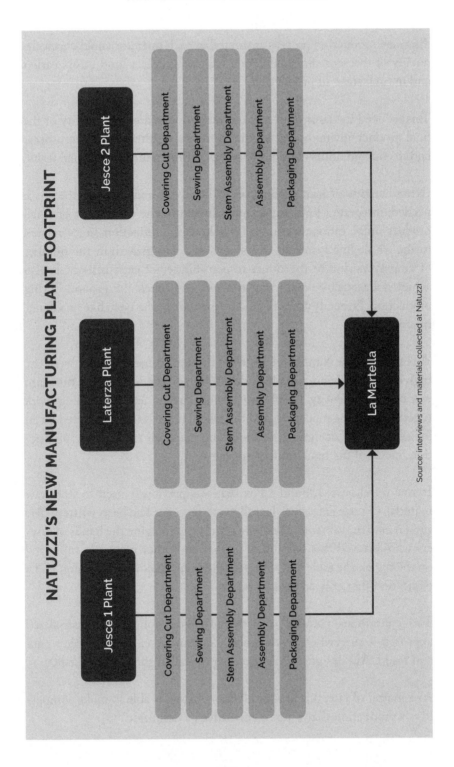

NATUZZI'S NEW MANUFACTURING PLANT FOOTPRINT

Jesce 1 Plant

Covering Cut Department
Sewing Department
Stem Assembly Department
Assembly Department
Packaging Department

Laterza Plant

Covering Cut Department
Sewing Department
Stem Assembly Department
Assembly Department
Packaging Department

Jesce 2 Plant

Covering Cut Department
Sewing Department
Stem Assembly Department
Assembly Department
Packaging Department

La Martella

Source: interviews and materials collected at Natuzzi

This new production process ensured that each operator could check the quality of the semi-finished goods, capturing defects and errors earlier and in each stage of production.

This reduced the time of execution but also increased the quality of the final product, giving operators the ability to see the production process end to end and understand how their part contributed to the final result.

Other benefits of lean production included the reduction of the space needed, integrated lines, ergonomics linked to the movement of small product units, rationalization of warehouses, production times related to the whole line localized in a single area, and growth in the number of employees due to the direct responsibilities of each activity. It also achieved Pasquale's dream that the sofa not touch the ground during production. Never. It floats from one operator to the next, like in a dancing movement.

When visiting a Natuzzi plant, what impressed me the most were the high levels of efficiency in all workstations and the feeling that the plant was one single entity. People are sewing, cutting and assembling work together with the machines, and the whole process is orchestrated by an invisible hand that moves the goods and materials through the production line until the final product appears.

In one warehouse, I found a box that was previously used to store raw material. On one side of it, the following sentence had been written: *"My work is now in your hands. Take care of it."* I can imagine the hands of sewers who received this box full of leather and other materials, inputting on the screen the code and then starting their work with a passion and a dedication that only artisans have.

This continuous paradox of artisanal production and industrialized approach is everywhere in the plant. You can see carpenters able to use and read CAD designs, while listening to Italian songs from the 50s.

As a matter of fact, this lean production system is able to make competitive a production that is not competitive by definition.

But in describing Natuzzi sofas, one cannot stop at the production process itself. There is something more. Through my interviews, I understood that a Natuzzi sofa is not only a sofa, it is something more.

Some people say that in the US, buying a Natuzzi is like buying an Apple product. But, knowing what goes on behind the scenes, the hours spent in R&D and in optimizing the whole process, the men and women involved in the production, the passion, the energy and all this, I understand there is a lot more in front of us than just a sofa.

The product itself is famous for its aesthetic and comfort. *"There are customers who sit on the sofa and customers who sit in the sofa. Natuzzi is able to make both happy,"*[123] Vito Basile said.

"When you see a Natuzzi sofa, it evokes in you a sense of comfort, a sense of softness. The beauty, the harmony. The need to lay down on it, into a warm embrace."

Thanks to the lean production line, it is managed by the expert hands of operators who sew it, prepare it, upholster it, assemble it and finally pack it, moving with each pass a piece of their history, of their sweat and their passion.

Natuzzi sofas transmit a sense of hospitality and harmony that you find when you visit the south of Italy and the area where Natuzzi values were born and developed. The same harmony is reflected in the choice of materials, colours and components in Natuzzi.

"Where people see an angle, Pasquale Natuzzi sees a curve."[124] This is a famous motto expressing the willingness of Pasqual to soften the edges, reduce the harshness of life and create a unique experience. Moreover, this is reflected in his style of leadership. He does not like conflict and always tends to smooth out a clash.

---

123 Vito Basile, interview performed in January 2017.
124 Renato Quaranta, interview performed in January 2017.

When you buy a Natuzzi sofa, you not only buy a product, you also buy the values of the company, the respect for people, the devotion to the customers, the time spent optimizing the process, the time spent searching for high quality materials, the strive for excellence that is embedded in its employees, the love for work and the desire to make the customer happy.

You buy the product of a company dedicated to a territory that also improves the lives of the people working for it.

You buy the ethics of the company that exports its standards across geographies, independent of local labour laws.

During my interviews, I was surprised at how many people were excited to share their experiences, to show their admiration for Pasquale's courage and determination, to show appreciation for their profession and, most importantly, the personal experiences they had with this company.

Old production process. Manual leather cutting

Old production process

The new Laterza manufacturing plant in Italy

New lean production process. Moving line

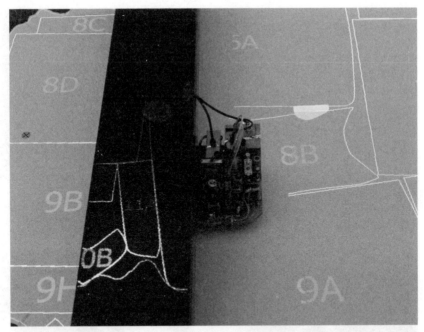

New production process. Scanning and digitization of the leather cutting

New production process. Digital nesting

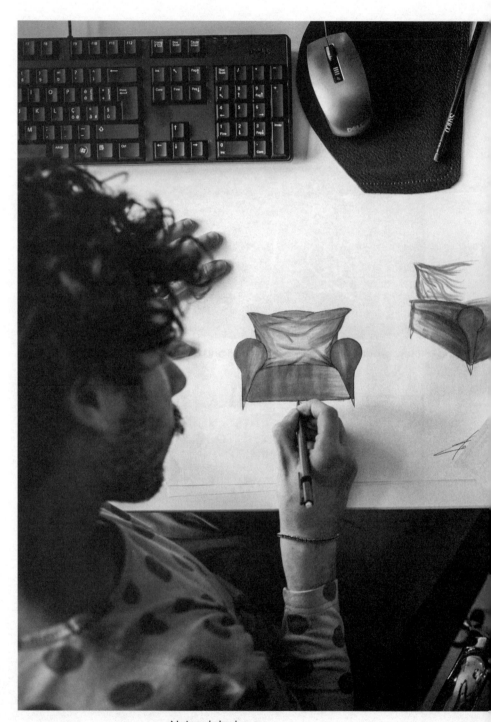

Natuzzi designers

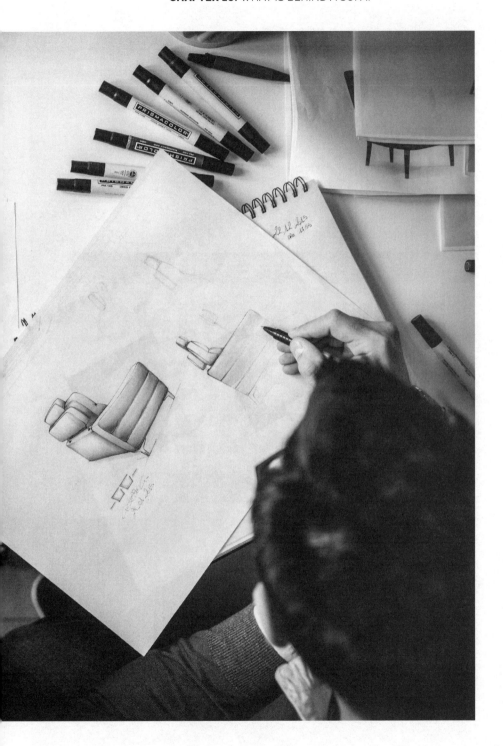

CHAPTER 11

THE BEATING HEART OF NATUZZI

Natuzzi is a paradox. An artisanal production transformed into a global, modern company, where machines and humans transfer the concept of beauty to their products.

I've illustrated how the production process has changed over the years, but what makes Natuzzi special is its beating heart: the Style Centre. There, more than 100 people scan the market, read, collect information and travel around the world to get new ideas, designs, techniques and skills. This department is where everything comes from.

Originally, Natuzzi's customers were the ones requesting certain types of models and colours, but over the years, this centre became the crux of the creative process in the company. Although Natuzzi offers a wide category of products for the living room, the market and the sofa are still the starting point.

Now, Natuzzi has two main brands: one in the upper segment (Natuzzi Italia) and one in the middle segment (Natuzzi Editions).

The company has clustered its customers into three categories:

• Bourgeois prosperity: more luxury
• Career and family: more traditional
• Sophisticated single

With the support of business intelligence, Natuzzi scans the market and collects information about these categories. An important role in this market screening is the fashion industry, setting new trends globally.

On the other side, the creative part of Natuzzi begins. Designers give their own interpretation of the trends, by creating what they call the 'masterpiece matrix', a set of combinations of colours, shapes and shades.

These matrixes are considered pieces of art at Natuzzi and pictures are stored year by year in the company archives. *"The masterpiece matrix is a suggestion, a way to match materials, colours and transfer the harmony concept.*

There's something magical in this process: as chemists they create the mood board in vitro, hoping this will become real in the shops,"[125] Vito Basile said.

Once the creative end is completed, the managerial part starts. Merchandisers identify which products are to be offered in each segment. A real ping-pong process begins between the two departments, since on one side there is the pure creative desire to transfer a concept to products, and on the other side the deep knowledge of the customers and their needs, which forces the team to recalibrate those choices to make them appealing.

In this process, external vendors also enter into the game. For certain products that are not produced internally (i.e., tables and lamps), absolute research on the materials is performed to make sure quality is at its best.

The result of this process is the release of the 'commercial matrix', a document where the combination of products, materials and colours is organized by customer segment.

All this work is performed using both internal and external designers, architects and visuals. The collaboration with external architects and partners helps Natuzzi remain open to what's new, rethink ways of doing things and get a fresh look from the outside.

These all help in shaping the collection that is launched each year. Today Natuzzi is like a fashion company and launches its new collection every year at the Milan Design International Fair in April. Natuzzi's collections are built around the sofa, matching and blending together shapes in a unique experience.

The collection designs made on paper are then transferred to the prototype developer to follow the process outlined in the previous chapter.

As in the past, exhibitions still have a crucial role in presenting the outcomes of the hard work done. Milan is still the main one internationally, where all key trends in living are launched.

Cosimo Bardi, head of the Natuzzi Style Centre, said *"Milan is a moment to show off, to explain the brand and its values and simply enthuse customers. This is not an easy moment, since the stylist is Pasquale, who has the role to safeguard the brand and its DNA. And in order to get a yes from him, we have to present many different models every time."*[126]

In addition to external fairs, the company has had its own showroom in Santeramo for many years. A 'retail congress' is organized every year, inviting Natuzzi retailers globally and presenting them with all the new models.

In this instance, the role of merchandiser is key. Together with the owners of Natuzzi shops, they have to translate the harmony concept of the set of products they are going to position locally. *"The big challenge we have today is in translating the harmony concept worldwide, since in shops owned by us we saw growth at double digits, while in those owned by third parties, they still have the last word on the products they want to position and sell."*[127]

You might think this process is a structured one. It is not. The main characteristic and also main challenge for external managers is the way of working: a mix of structured and completely unstructured work, based on the experience and insights of the employees, and finally of Pasquale.

"If you don't experience this, you cannot understand. Choices that normal companies would make based on data and analysis are here done on the fly. As an example, Pasquale decided to launch beds in just three months in 2014. We never produced beds, and we had no clue how to do it in all the countries where we operate. How big, how tall ... all these questions were unanswered at that moment. But the intuitiveness of Pasquale pushed us to do that and in one year we made an additional $5 million US in revenue!"[128]

Pasquale is a volcano of ideas, and the role of his people is to make them real.

---

125 Vito Basile, interview performed in September 2017.

126 Cosimo Bardi, Natuzzi Head of Style center, interview performed in September 2017.

127 Ibid.

128 Ibid.

Example of *"Natuzzi's Masterpiece matrix"*

Example of *"Natuzzi's Masterpiece matrix"*

CHAPTER 12

THE HARMONY-DRIVEN FUTURE

"We've been in this market for 50 years and we want to stay for 500 years more."[129]

Since its beginning, Natuzzi has experienced at least three revolutions.

The first one was the massive production to satisfy the American market. The second was the creation of its own distribution channel and expanding the market in other regions to better differentiate the business. The third was the brand revolution and moving from a manufacturer to a retailer.

In all these years, the story of the company and its founder, Pasquale Natuzzi, are strongly interconnected. This is a story around the search for beauty and harmony in all aspects: outside the company, with a product coming from the market for the market; inside the company, with a passion for his people and with a tendency to strive for excellence; and around the company, with a responsibility that goes beyond the financial results.

The search for colours, the selection of materials, the combination of different furniture components, the attention to details and the design of all its curves are orchestrated by an invisible hand that aims to achieve and create a harmony in the environment.

Pasquale has been defined as a warlord, a methodical man, an undiscovered Italian gem, different from the average Italian industrialists, the rare case of a person where creativity and common sense are in perfect balance, a visionary, a lean thinker of the 90s, the entrepreneur of the south of Italy giving work to the north of Italy, a dreamer, an optimist and a forerunner of industrial humanism.

What is clear is the strong influence the leader had and still has today in writing the company's future. The most challenging part is consolidating the brand. The brand allows customers to identify a product and attribute values that transcend the product itself.

---

129 Pasquale Natuzzi, analyst call, April 2008.

"It is something that resides in the mind of the consumer, a perceptual entity, rooted in reality, but that also reflects the perceptions and consumer idiosyncrasies and therefore creates in the mind of the consumer a range of emotions that lead him to choose or not the system offered. The evocative power of the brand is carried out completely when the consumer recognizes the product's existence and that entire world as it drew."[130]

Although Natuzzi is a strong and solid company, its main challenge for the future is in the ability to transpose its values – its DNA – into the brand.

The ongoing investments in R&D, together with those in advertising, are helping this along.

Further potential exists in leveraging CSR in the brand strategy. A transformation in marketing is already happening.

"Over the past 60 years, marketing has moved from being product-centric (Marketing 1.0) to being consumer-centric (Marketing 2.0).

"Today we see marketing as transforming once again in response to the new dynamics in the environment. We see companies expanding their focus from products to consumers to humankind issues.

"Marketing 3.0 is the stage when companies shift from consumer-centricity to human-centricity and where profitability is balanced with corporate responsibility."[131]

The new generations are focused more and more on the ethical aspects of a brand and, as shared in previous chapters, Natuzzi has a strong commitment to this and can leverage it to further position its brand. A holistic approach to sustainability, corporate donations and brand communication strategy can boost this positioning. But apart from this, today the company has a strong organization and strong people to drive the change.

Pasquale has an exceptional ability to energize people. His vision to transform Natuzzi from a manufacturing company into a retailer has been successful, as shown by the company's recent financial results. He has a dream of creating a real end-to-end company, starting with the customer and identifying their needs and going back to the customer with products and services that make them happy.

His determination, patience and know-how will pay off. The potential for further growth is there, especially as the global market overcomes the current crisis, and as the middle class begins to invest again in their homes and furniture.

Based on what I discovered about Natuzzi, I believe in a positive and bright future for this company.

"If there is no passion, you cannot realize anything. You must believe in the product you are creating and put all your efforts towards doing your best. Only in this way can the product be yours. Otherwise, it will always be something external to you,"[132] Antonio Ventricelli said.

Mr Pasquale Natuzzi will never give up. This is clear.

But his employees are also sure they will not give up. They have enough love, passion, ideas and dedication to make Natuzzi a brand that lasts for the next 500 years.

During an interview with one employee I asked the question, "What would you ask Pasquale Natuzzi today?"

The employee immediately replied:

"Mr Natuzzi, shall we start?"

---

130 Keller K.L., Strategic brand management, Prentice Hall, Upper Saddle River, New Jersey, 2003.

131 Kotler P., Armstrong G. , *Principles of Marketing*, 16th Edition, Pearson, 2016.

132 Antonio Ventricelli, interview performed in January 2017.

AN INTRODUCTION TO LUCA CONDOSTA

Luca Condosta is Group Vice President Finance at ABB. He has 15 years of experience in multinationals, and a passion for business and leadership. He has written several papers on corporate governance and corporate strategy and published his first book in 2008 on sustainability reporting.